The Nurse's Calling

THE NURSE'S CALLING

A Christian Spirituality of Caring for the Sick

Mary Elizabeth O'Brien

PAULIST PRESS
New York/Mahwah, N.J.

Cover design by Kokopelli Design Studio

Type design by IRONAPPLE

All cover images are royalty free, from Comstock

Library of Congress Cataloging-in-Publication Data

O'Brien, Mary Elizabeth.
    The nurse's calling : a Christian spirituality of caring for the sick / Mary Elizabeth O'Brien.
    p.   cm.
    ISBN 0-8091-4009-8
    1. Nursing—Religious aspects—Christianity. 2. Nursing ethics. 3. Christian life. 4. Caring—Religious aspects—Christianity. I. Title.

RT85.2 .O367 2001
610.73—dc21

                                             00-051686

Published by Paulist Press
997 Macarthur Boulevard
Mahwah, N.J. 07430

www.paulistpress.com

Printed and bound in the
United States of America

CONTENTS

Dedication

For all Christian nurses who commit their heart and their hands to caring for the ill in the name of Jesus.

THE SACRED COVENANT:
A Nurse's Prayer

Gentle God,

You alone are the source of my strength and the
center of my life;
bless my nursing that it may always
be guided by the sacred covenant
of Your loving care.

Use me as Your instrument in serving the sick:

use my eyes to look with compassion on those
who are broken in body or in spirit;

use my hands to touch with tenderness those
who suffer illness or injury;

use my lips to speak words of comfort to those
who are anxious or afraid.

Dear Lord,

Let me recognize every sickroom as a tabernacle where
You dwell;

and

let me never forget, as I care for the ill, that

the ground on which I am standing is holy,

the vocation to which I am called

is holy.

Help me to be worthy.

Sister Mary Elizabeth O'Brien, Ph.D., R.N., F.A.A.N.

INTRODUCTION

This book was conceived during course work for a master of theological studies degree. After almost two decades as a nurse researcher and nurse educator, I decided to undertake a sojourn on the other side of the desk. The catalyst for my decision was the completion of nursing research on the psychosocial and spiritual needs of persons living with life-threatening illnesses. During the study, participants spoke poignantly about their spiritual and religious needs and beliefs. Professional nurse-caregivers shared their spiritual concerns as well. Both groups posed faith-related questions that I felt ill equipped to discuss. While confident that I possessed strong religious beliefs, the quest for "faith seeking understanding" captivated my spirit.

Early on in my theology program I elected to study topics dealing with spirituality and care of the sick. One of my greatest joys was derived from participating in scripture courses, which afforded me the opportunity to relate the teachings, especially those of Jesus recorded in the New Testament, to my calling as a nurse. In a New Testament course I examined the healing activities of Jesus; I explored scripturally the concept of Christ as role model in caring for the sick. Old Testament studies focused my thinking on the theme of covenant; how God's commitment to care for his people could be understood in describing the nurse-patient relationship.

In the following pages I have tried to share some thoughts on favorite scripture passages from both Old and New Testaments that might be meaningful to the Christian nurse. I have also included anecdotes derived from my clinical experience and the experiences of other Christian nurses that interpret the scriptures as lived out in the nurse's calling. Direct quotations were elicited during interviews with a cadre of contemporary practicing nurses; pseudonyms are used whenever nurses are named.

Each chapter is organized according to a particular scriptural theme. In the first chapter the nurse's vocation is envisioned as flowing from and supported by Jesus' teaching that a *cup of cold water* be given in his name to all who thirst (Matthew 10:42). Chapter two describes nursing as a ministry, because as St. Paul so eloquently asserted, each person (each nurse) holds within his or her *earthen vessel-ness* the *treasure* of God's love (2 Corinthians 4:7). Chapter three, which explores the nurse's role as healer, has as its scriptural model Luke's description of the woman healed by *touching* Jesus' garment (Luke 8:43). In the fourth chapter comfort for the nurse in difficult times is derived from the beautiful passage in Isaiah that promises God's care amidst *raging waters* (43:2). In chapter five God's promise of *eagle's wings* reflects from whence comes the nurse's strength (Isaiah 40:31). Chapter six describes the rewards of nursing the sick in terms of *treasures which are stored up in heaven* (Matthew 6:20–21). Chapter seven addresses nursing's call to reverence the sacredness of human life (John 10:10). And, in chapter eight the spirituality of the nurse is placed where it may be crafted into a thing of grace and beauty; in the *hands of the Divine Potter* (Jeremiah 18:1–6).

I express heartfelt appreciation to those who inspired and reviewed the original manuscript with commitment and care. Judy Shelly planted the conceptual seed for the book and lovingly nourished its growth with her support, encouragement and critique. Elizabeth McFarlane gently and caringly evaluated the text in light of her personal spirituality of nursing; and Sister Mary Hartnett painstakingly reviewed each page for clinical, as well as spiritual relevance.

I am also especially grateful to Father Joseph Scott of Paulist Press for shepherding the manuscript to publication with a light but careful touch.

Ultimately I acknowledge my greatest gratitude to God, the source of my strength, the center of my life and the true author of this work. In my immensely fragile "earthen-vesselness," His word is a *"lamp for my feet and a light for my path"* (Psalm 119:105). To God the Father, to his son our Lord Jesus, and to the Holy Spirit, I give loving and reverent thanks.

CHAPTER 1.
A CUP OF COLD WATER:

The Nurse's Calling

"And whoever gives only a cup of cold water in my name to one of these little ones...he will surely not lose his reward."
                                    —Matthew 10:42

In a pastoral letter written nearly two thousand years ago Saint Paul reminded the early Christians that they had been called by God to a "holy life...according to...the grace bestowed on [them] in Christ Jesus before time began" (2 Timothy 1:9). Contemporary Christian nurses are called to a holy life as well. They are called to support, called to nurture, called to comfort, called to console, called to serve. Christian nurses are called, in the course of their practice, to give to each patient a *cup of cold water* in the name of Jesus. That is the heart of the Christian nurse's calling; that is the blessing of the Christian nurse's calling.

This is not an easy time to be a nurse. "Managed care" is in; "fee for service" is out. Health care systems are operating with financially constrained budgets, and when cost reduction is mandated nursing is often one of the first services affected. As an academician I learn of the impact of such budgetary cuts on patient care from former students, now staff nurses and nurse managers in a variety of health care settings. They express frustration at not having time to provide care in the manner they were taught during their academic programs. They are concerned that they will be required to focus on simply getting the work done rather than on truly caring for patients. They worry about moral and ethical issues associated with certain of the technological advances in medicine and health care. And they wonder, a few of them, if they really did the right thing by entering a caregiving profession. It is for these nurses especially that I wanted to write about the *nurse's calling*, about the *Christian spirituality of caring for the sick*.

Perhaps the thoughts and experiences I have chosen to share will seem idealistic in this era of sophisticated health care. The gospel message of Jesus is idealistic, yet it has survived escalating levels of knowledge and technology for almost two millennia. This is because the gospel of Jesus touches the heart. The message is simple but profound. We, as members of the human family, are called to care, called to love. Our greatest commandment is taught by Jesus; we must love God and love one another (Matthew 22:37–39). And we, as nurses, are called to care, called to love, in a special way, those who are who are ill in their bodies, in their minds or in their spirits. We, as Christian nurses, are called to love as Jesus loved, without discrimination, without reserve and sometimes without reward. We are called to follow him to the cross, if need be, in order to live out this vocation of loving.

Speaking on the occasion of an annual "White Mass" honoring the health care professions, at Saint Patrick's Cathedral in New York, His Eminence John Cardinal O'Connor likened the Christian calling to care for the sick to the priestly vocation. His Eminence observed that while he was conducting an ordination ceremony the previous day he had reflected on the concept of consecration as applied to health care providers:

I couldn't help but think of the similarity because, in a very real way, you are consecrated. There is a beautiful portion of today's gospel that speaks of consecration, and I think it is as pertinent to you in health care as it is to priests and bishops. Our Lord is talking to his Father at the Last Supper, and he says of his apostles, "I gave them your word, and the world has hated them for it; they do not belong to the world, any more than I belong to the world. I do not ask you to take them out of the world, but to guard them from the evil one. They are not of the world, any more than I am of the world. Consecrate them by means of truth."

John 17:14–17[1]

His Eminence added:

As Christians we are consecrated, set apart....We live in the world and have obligations to the world, yet [Christ] has taken us out of the world and consecrated us to himself.[2]

It is an immense challenge for nurses to practice a Christian spirituality and a Christian consecration of caring for the sick in today's world, yet it is a glorious challenge as well. We are gifted with the opportunity to respond to Christ's call over and over again each day. Cardinal O'Connor described the importance of a caregiver's personal spirituality from the perspective of his extensive ministry to those living with the human immunodeficiency virus:

When I visited many hundreds of persons with AIDS, I discovered something that has been infinitely more important to them than any physical or medical help we can give them: the opportunity to talk about their own spiritual state, the opportunity to talk about their fears and anxieties, their hope for the future....A doctor or a nurse can do so much to help relieve such anxieties by spiritual example...[and by] treating people with spiritual gentleness.[3]

In the following pages are included some splendid stories of nurses who exemplify the lived experience of Jesus' gospel message; who indeed treat their patients, as His Eminence taught, with *spiritual gentleness.* Their lives inspire me, strengthen me and give me hope. They affirm for me the fact that no matter how our health care system develops or changes, nursing will never lose its heart: its heart of love; its heart of caring and its heart of compassion; its heart modeled on the heart of Jesus, the Healer of all hearts.

The Nurse's Calling

Margaret, an oncology nurse with fifteen years of clinical experience, described her practice as encompassing a spiritual calling:

> I really feel I was called by God to be a nurse; that is the way I am to serve Christ. In this relationship being the "handmaiden of the Lord" is in no way demeaning; it's a gift. Who better can you serve than Christ? Nursing is a call to a working partnership with God, with Christ, and a working partnership with your patients. It's a call to trust and caring: of your trusting that God placed that patient in your hands so you can serve as his instrument, and of the patient's trusting that you will care for him with Christ's love and compassion.

From the time of Jesus, Christian nursing of the sick has been guided by a spiritual call to care. This spiritual ministry was directed especially toward care of the poor and the vulnerable: *"For I was...ill and you cared for me....Amen, I say to you, whatever you did for one of these least brothers of mine, you did for me"* (Matthew 25:35–36, 40).

Jesus was teaching his disciples that caring for the sick was a task especially dear to his heart. Imagine for a moment the power and the beauty of Jesus' call for us as nurses. *Whatever you did*...a cup of water to quench a parched throat, a medication to alleviate painful suffering, a comforting word to ease the anxiety of a fearful patient...*you did for me*. There is a lovely anecdote told of St. Elizabeth of Hungary, a thirteenth-century patroness of nursing. It is reported that after she had cared for many of the poor and infirm, Elizabeth was heard to say to those assisting her: "How well it is for us that thus we bathe and care for our Lord."[4] It is this spirituality of caring from which the Christian nurse's call is derived, as expressed so articulately by Margaret in describing her practice.

The concept of a spiritual calling is currently being explored by many individuals in our society. Books, articles and films abound on varying aspects of spirituality or the spiritual nature of the human person. The nursing community is also reflecting, through research and publications, a renewed interest in the spiritual needs of patients and families, as well as the personal spirituality and spiritual vocation of the nurse. A recent literature review linking the concepts of *spirituality* and *nursing* documented publication of over four hundred English-language journal articles on the topic in the past five years. The meaning of the term *spirituality*, however, needs to be explored as to its use in relation to the nurse's role in general, and in regard to the calling of the Christian nurse in particular.

A Christian Spirituality of Nursing

Approaching the topic of the spirituality of nursing in contemporary society is both difficult and critically important. In this era of sophisticated philosophies of care and highly advanced medical technology, nurses may be faced with practice-related issues that pose serious moral and ethical dilemmas. These problems must be dealt with in light of the nurse's personal spiritual and religious beliefs. It is vital for today's practitioner of nursing, whether clinician, educator, administrator or researcher, to have a well-grounded understanding of his or her spiritual and religious tradition.

Attempting to define the concept of spirituality in relation to current nursing literature is fraught with complexity. There are myriad conceptualizations describing goals, philosophies of life or norms of behavior that some define as spirituality; religious beliefs are sometimes excluded in these worldviews. The distinction between the terms *spirituality* and *religion* is an important one, since the two concepts are sometimes used interchangeably within the nursing community. In a widely cited nursing literature review of definitions of spirituality and religion, Julia Emblen highlights the distinction between the concepts. In definitions of spirituality, she reported that nine terms appear most often: *"personal, life, principle, animator, being, God, quality, relationship* and *transcendent."*[5] The words most frequently associated with definitions of religion were: *"system, beliefs, organized, person, worship, practices."*[6] In a more recent review of the nursing literature Dyson, Cobb and Forman found that the key elements in spirituality definitions included the terms *"self, others* and *God";*[7] and Bernice Golberg's exploration of nursing's understanding of spirituality revealed emphasis placed on the phenomena of *"meaning, presencing, empathy/compassion, giving hope, love, religion/transcendence, touch* and *healing."*[8] Finally, Margaret Burkhardt, also a theorist of spirituality in nursing, asserted that "at the essence of being, spirituality manifests in relationships with one's self, others, nature and a divine being or life force."[9]

As can be seen from the above positions, a multiplicity of concepts are currently being associated with the term *spirituality* within the nursing community. For the Christian nurse, however, spirituality has a distinct meaning as articulated by theologian Joann Conn: "For Christians [spirituality] means one's entire life as understood, felt, imagined and decided upon in relationship to God, in Christ Jesus, empowered by the Spirit."[10] It is from the gospel message of Jesus that nurses derive their mission to care for the sick, their modeling of how that caring should be carried out and their understanding of the inherent sacredness of their work.

As with the concept of spirituality, the term *nursing* is currently defined broadly to incorporate such varied dimensions of the profession as hospital care, outpatient care, emergency care, home care and community health care. In her book *Nursing: The Finest Art,* historian Patricia Donahue asserts that "nursing has been called the oldest of the arts and the youngest of the professions."[11] Nursing has consistently been viewed as both a science and an art. Nursing science consists of the theoretical knowledge base that undergirds practice; nursing art may be viewed as "the creative application" of this knowledge in caring for patients and families.[12] Caring is generally described in the nursing literature as the central concept of and basis for professional practice.[13] Similarly, in theological literature the nurse is viewed as a symbol of caring. Thus it is suggested that "it is not surprising to find Moses, and, by implication, God spoken of as a nurse (Numbers 11:12).[14]

Most nurses have a spiritual philosophy of life that undergirds their caring for the sick. The Christian nurse receives her mandate to care for the ill and the infirm directly from Christ's teaching of the brotherhood of all persons. Jesus preached that life, which is sacred, is to be lived in accordance with the will of his Father and under the direction of the Spirit. Thus the nurse will carry out her professional role as a disciple of Jesus, in relationship with the Father and guided by the inspiration of the Holy Spirit.

A Cup of Water

Megan, a master's-prepared hospice nurse, described her understanding of the *cup of cold water* scripture:

> You can give a *cup of cold water* in whatever you do as a nurse by loving people. You can always draw patients to the Lord by letting Jesus' love flow through you to them. And by seeing Jesus in them. That is the *cup of cold water:* you did it in my name, you did it unto me.

The *cup of cold water* teaching was directed to all of Jesus' disciples—those who would be his representatives after the Resurrection.[15] Jesus' identification of water as the liquid in the proverbial cup may be interpreted in both a literal and symbolic way. Water is essential to the survival of the human person. Our bodies are approximately 60 percent water; and most of us cannot live more than a few days without drinking water. When patients are recovering from surgery or a serious illness, one of the first things their bodies crave is water. Water calms our spirits as well. Sitting by the ocean or a mountain lake refreshes our souls. I have, on occasion, during times of stress or fatigue, found myself saying: "I need to go and be by the water." Water has spiritually restorative power, especially for those of us whose professional and family lives are centered primarily in urban areas.

Water is also a scriptural symbol. Water was used as a symbol of life in both Old and the New Testaments. God is described in Jeremiah 2:13 as the *"source of living waters"*; and in the New Testament, baptism with water is the sign of salvation.[16] The "cup of cold water" scripture passage is part of what has been described as the "mission discourse of Jesus"; that is, Jesus' sending forth of his disciples to carry out the gospel message.[17] Thus the scripture well supports the Christian nurse's call to minister.

The "cup of cold water" ministry is also reflected scripturally in Jesus' care for people's ordinary physical needs. As Matthew tells us, his *"heart was moved with pity"* when he saw a crowd of hungry, tired followers waiting for him at the end of a day. Although the disciples would have sent the group home, Jesus told them: *"There is no need for them to go away; give them some food yourselves."* And, with Jesus' blessing, five loaves and two fishes were multiplied to feed the crowd of five thousand (Matthew 14:14–21).

During an internship in hospital chaplaincy, which I served as part of my theology program, a member of our department of spiritual ministry introduced me to what he labeled: "'the cup of cold water' ministry." There may be times, he said, when the best way you can minister is to literally get a glass of cold water for someone. If a patient you are visiting is feverish and thirsty, it's not the time to pull out your Bible and start reading scripture. Give them a cup of water in Jesus' name; that is spiritual ministry at that moment.

I had the chance to practice the "'cup of cold water' ministry" one afternoon when the pediatric oncology clinic to which I had been assigned was, in truth, chaotic. The clinic was short-staffed that day, and there were several patient emergencies. I had been a nurse for many years but was new to pastoral care and not yet secure in my role. I was well received by the medical and nursing staff; nevertheless I remained timid about carrying out ministerial activities when the clinic was so busy. As a nurse I was sensitive to not interfering with the many nursing activities critical to supporting the children's chemotherapy.

As I hovered hesitantly in the doorway of one of the chemo treatment rooms, I overheard a nurse—in the process of initiating therapy for a seven-year-old with leukemia—say to another nurse who was wrestling with an HIV-positive toddler: "Timmy asked for milk about ten minutes ago but I just can't get to it." That was my cue! I jumped into the conversation, delighted for the opportunity and said: "I'll get it for him."

Aside from quenching Timmy's thirst, I think this small task serendipitously helped cement my acceptance as the clinic chaplain. As I rushed out the door on my search-and-rescue mission for milk, I heard one of the nurses stage-whisper: "A chaplain who runs errands; we'll keep her!"

The moral of my story, of course, is that in this time of major health care reform, with so many facilities experiencing skeletonlike staffing patterns and early discharge agendas, nurses may have little time to sit and listen to or pray with patients. The nurse can, however, carry out the most ordinary of tasks—the serving of a *cup of cold water*, a glass of juice, a carton of milk—with the love and the care and the gentleness of Jesus. During a conversation with an ICU patient in a major urban medical center, I asked if she felt that she was being well cared for by the nursing staff. The patient responded: "Well, I know that they are very short-staffed in this unit (it's interesting that a *patient* had so quickly picked up a term from nursing lingo: *short-staffed*); the nurses are spread pretty thin and they don't always answer your call bell right away, but," she asserted, "I know that the nurses in this ICU really care about you, and caring goes a very long way with me."

While it is, in fact, during the carrying out of the ordinary activities of the day that one may be serving the *cup of cold water*, most nurses are unaware or only minimally aware of the impact of their actions and interactions on patients and families. A few years ago a friend underwent radical cancer surgery at a local hospital. The surgical intervention was followed by months of aggressive but effective chemotherapy. I promised to be there through the treatment sessions.

The intravenous chemotherapy "cocktail" prescribed was so potentially toxic that my friend had to be hospitalized for several days with each treatment. We were both nurses with many years of clinical experience. In this stressful health care situation, however, we were simply *patient* and *family*. This was the first time I had the opportunity to appreciate a nurse's caring from the other side of the fence. Each time we called to schedule a hospital admission, our first question was: "Who's on '7–3' the day of treatment?"; "Who's on evenings?"; "Who's on nights?" Of course the questions in our hearts were: "Will there be nurses on duty who understand how frightening the chemotherapy process is for patients and families? Will there be nurses who care enough to go the extra mile to make the experience a little less traumatic? Will there be nurses who care for us as they would want to be cared for?"

Near the end of a year-long series of treatments the staff had gotten the measure of this patient-family team and began to laughingly ask if we would like an advance copy of the oncology unit staffing sheets prior to scheduling a procedure? Both I, as surrogate family, and my nurse friend, as patient, received lots of *cups of cold water* during the chemotherapy experience. Nurses stopped by to ask how things were going, even if they didn't seem to be going so well on a particular day. They understood how stressful the therapy was, regardless of our nursing backgrounds. Nurses teased and laughed with us to lighten the mood when it seemed that one more treatment might be just too much to handle. The oncology staff nurses let us know that they cared, and they accepted our caring in return. Sacred bonds, sacred covenants were established during that experience—sacred relationships that I treasure to this day.

A Sacred Covenant

So tiny, so fragile, the small patient seems; almost lost amidst the wires and lines and monitoring devices which furnish her neonatal intensive care home. A miniature hand reaches out desperately seeking comfort in this strange new world into which the frail newborn has entered. Tenderly a NICU nurse allows the tiny fist to grasp her hand, to make a human connection, to make a spiritual connection. This is the nurse-patient covenant; this is a sacred covenant.

In a book entitled *Spirituality in Nursing: Standing on Holy Ground*, I introduced the conceptualization of nursing as encompassing a *sacred covenant*.[18] The concept, which presents a spiritual perspective on the nurse-patient relationship, was derived from interviews with practitioners of nursing, including nurse-clinicians, nurse-administrators, nurse-educators and nurse-researchers. One of the interviewees, Carol, a nurse-anesthesiologist with eighteen years of experience in her field, explained the spiritual dimension that she understood as part of her covenantal relationship with perioperative patients:

> I try to talk to patients when they arrive in the O.R. suite. They are just scared to death. I might be the last person to talk to them before they go to sleep. I listen to their concerns. I listen to see if they say anything like "I'm in God's hands," and then I just take it from there. I say: "It's OK to put all your trust in God; he'll be with you in there [O.R.]." I reassure them of God's love and care during the surgery. This is when people are at their most vulnerable. This is the most logical time to think of God. I pray silently while the patient is under anesthesia; if they're having a hard time, I ask God to give them strength.[19]

While there are many Old Testament references to God's covenantal caring, such as Yahweh's commitment to the people of Israel,[20] the Christian incarnational theology of the New Testament represents the completion of the covenant between

God and man. In discussing the concept of covenant for Christian lawyers, Joseph Allegretti observes that "Jesus is the fulfillment of the Old Testament promise to the Israelites."[21]

I have made a covenant, a spiritual commitment, God says to His people; trust me for I will care for you (Psalm 81:3–4). I have made a covenant, a spiritual commitment, the nurse may say to a patient; trust me for I will care for you. The nurse's covenant is reflected in the words of the Nightingale Oath of old: *"I solemnly pledge myself before God...[to] devote myself to the welfare of those committed to my care."*[22] A covenantal theme is also included in Franciscan Sister Mary Berenice Beck's classic "Nurse's Prayer": *"I am Thine Own, great Healer, help Thou me to serve Thy sick in humble charity. I ask not thanks or praise but only light, to care for them in every way aright. My charges, sick and well, they all are Thine."*[23]

Henri Nouwen observed that the concept of covenant means an "unconditional commitment to be of service."[24] The principle of faithful service is also described as central to nurse-patient covenantal relationships,[25] as is the transcendent nature of the care-giving relationship.[26] The nurse-patient covenant is a partnership of trust based on the spiritual nature of the care-giving relationship. Franciscan physician Daniel Sulmasy comments that the "spiritual doctor or nurse...enters into relationships of trust with patients." This process requires faith in the "basic goodness" of the healing relationship.[27] The importance of both the trust and faithfulness inherent in the nurse-patient covenant is described by a registered nurse with a six-year history of caring for maintenance hemodialysis patients:

> Kidney disease is a really difficult condition to deal with. Patients are so dependent on the caregivers. Their caregiver is their means to life. The nurse is really sustaining their lives. While the patient is on dialysis the nurse could cause that patient's death. Patients might see the physician once or twice a week, but the nurse is there all the time. The nurse is responsible for that patient's life and for that patient's being able to go home.[28]

The Christian nurse has the opportunity to continue the covenantal commitment that the Father began in sending his Son to heal the brokenness of the world. The sacredness of the nurse-patient relationship provides the forum for the nurse to become a symbol of Christ's faithfulness in responding to the Father's mission: *Not my will but Thine be done.* This faithfulness is manifested in the daily living out of the commitment to care and to love as Jesus taught and modeled in his life on earth.

Anne Marie, a baccalaureate-prepared nurse-clinician, described her perception of the covenantal relationship with patients for a Christian nurse:

> I think the longer you work in nursing the more you see it as a ministry, as a covenant with Christ and with your patient. It's a privilege. It's the closest thing I have found to the sacred; the relationship, the sharing you have with patients. It's trying to reach out and help patients and becoming personally touched by their struggle.

It's Christ within you that is making these deeper connections, these covenants that are spiritual, that are sacred.

"As I Have Loved You"

A Nurse's Tears

> *"I give you a new commandment: love one another. As I have loved you, so you also should love one another. This is how all will know that you are my disciples, if you have love for one another."*
>
> John 13:34

How the Christian nurse enters into a sacred covenant of caring will be determined by his or her personal spirituality and life history. Nurse-theorist Simone Roach suggests that caring for patients is an "art form" for the nurse: "...caring is shaped by what has transformed (the nurse) in her life experience, and by what she has learned and experienced within a particular professional role."[29] Each nurse's artistry will be developed and honed in the continual commitment to caring in the context of the specific and unique needs and concerns of the patients and families with whom she interacts.

Henri Nouwen observed that "one of the most compelling qualities of life in the spirit of Jesus is that we are always being sent out to bring...the gifts of God to...all peoples."[30] Nurses are great gift givers. I think it's something we do as a foil to the pain and suffering that are part and parcel of our chosen ministry. In the carrying out of treatments or the administering of medications we are sometimes forced to inflict pain or discomfort; thus we look for opportunities to bring joy in order to balance the negative aspects of our work.

One Christmas season I helped with a hospital project to provide clothing and gifts for needy patients and their families. Each nursing unit adopted several families. The staff got information about the age, size, gender and even special wishes of each family member. And the shopping sprees began! The nurses, especially those who were moms, delighted in finding clothing and children's toys that were recommended by their own little ones. Gifts for the adults were practical yet special so that they would fulfill the desires hesitantly shared by some of the needy families. During the week before Christmas there was a steady stream of staff nurses into the hospital boardroom, the project's "control central," bearing beautifully wrapped packages carefully labeled with notes of Christmas blessing for their recipients. The joy of the gift bearers was evident. They delighted in relating stories of how they had searched for a particular item: how excited they were on finding just the right toy for six-year-old Michael or the perfect warm sweater for eighty-seven-year-old Mrs. Smith. Nurses are gift givers.

I find an important connection uniting Jesus' comment that his disciples should have *love for one another*, Henri Nouwen's thought that Christians are called to bring God's gifts to others and the concept of nurses as gift givers. The gifts given by the nurses participating in the hospital Christmas project represented a lovely sense of attention to the material needs of others. Far greater, however, is the gift of self, which a nurse is asked to give many times during each working day. It may be physically fatiguing to carry out therapeutic procedures or to cope with a mountain of medical forms or computerized paperwork, but it is the emotional investment associated with these activities that truly reflects the nurse's gift—that reflects a nurse's caring.

Some years ago I worked as a staff nurse on a unit designated for renal-failure patients. One evening one of our favorite long-term patients "coded" during hemodialysis, and the physicians were unable to resuscitate her. She was a middle-aged mother with a delightful, outgoing personality. After a nurse had finished assessing her condition during rounds, she would always counter with: "Now tell me how things are going with you?" Her death was unexpected and a shock. She was not one of the patients who was *supposed* to die, at least not yet. The impact on the staff was powerful and many of us had tears in our eyes when the family arrived in response to an emergency phone call. As the unit charge nurse, I caught no small amount of "flack" from an evening supervisor who questioned whether it was professional to allow my staff to display their tears or to display my own tears, for that matter, in front of the family.

A few weeks after her funeral our staff received a letter of appreciation from the patient's family. The adult children told us how devastated they had been because they were not present at the death of their beloved mother. "But," they wrote, "we were comforted to arrive at Mother's hospital room and find her nurses with tears in their eyes. It meant so much to know that our mother died surrounded by nurses who loved her." The letter concluded: "We will never forget you."

A nurse's tears are sometimes the only and yet the most important gift of self she can give. Other caring activities may be forgotten by patients and families, but a nurse's tears tend to linger long in their memories.

Nursing—The Gospel Imperative

Beatitudes for Nurses

The word *gospel* is derived from the Greek word *evangelion* meaning "good news." The gospel of the New Testament refers to the "good news preached by Jesus that the Kingdom of God is at hand and the good news of what God has done on behalf of humanity in Jesus."[31] The gospel contains the "central content of Christian revelation; the glad tidings of the redemption."[32] The gospel Jesus preached contains an absolute and a radical message to those who would follow him. The mandates demand much from the Christian disciple: to care for the widow and the orphan, to feed the hungry and care for the sick, to love one's enemies, to do good to those who hate you, to turn the other cheek—over and over again, if one is to be a follower of Jesus. Brother Roger of Taize observes that we are not "built naturally for living the radicalization of the gospel," yet he explains that it is only "through giving ourselves totally that we grow": "What if your ground has become overgrown with thorns, scrub and briars. Christ lights a fire with the thorns: *Weakness becomes a crucible where the yes is made and remade and made again day after day.*"[33]

Several nurses described their vocational call in terms of the gospel mandate to serve. Pattie, a baccalaureate-prepared nurse with five years of experience in psych-mental health care, asserted:

> In my nursing I try to see the presence of God in everything I do—in my service to patients. It's the gospel service we are all called to. Like Jesus said: "When you do anything for the little ones." I actually feel that Christ is using me as an instrument; that's the importance of my spirituality. It's the most important aspect of my nursing.

Ann, a home care nurse for over fourteen years explained:

> I feel that my life in nursing is a gift—the call from Christ's gospel to care for the sick and the infirm. This

work with patients really deepens my faith; it deepens my wanting to live that gospel call.

And, Marie, a family nurse practitioner, shared her belief that because nursing had now come of age as a profession, nurses could admit to their spiritual vocation:

> A long time ago nurses were spiritual people, and then there was the push to make us a profession, to make us scientific. I think we sort of lost our spiritual side. But now nurses are realizing that we need to go back and look at what nursing really is, the art of nursing, the spirituality of nursing. It's more than just the medical aspects of care. The vocation of nursing is the caring part, the heart part. That's our gospel calling.

Now that we are secure in being professional, that will give us back the permission to be compassionate!

One evening, during my theology studies, I attended a eucharistic liturgy at a Franciscan house where a number of classmates and professors resided. At the conclusion of a homily on the Sermon on the Mount the priest celebrant looked around at the small group assembled for Mass and said quietly, "If someone who was not a follower of Christ asked: 'How can I know from your life that you are a Christian?', what would you answer?" The question was profound and challenging. And I wondered at the time how I would respond if someone asked me, "How can I know from your life that you are a Christian nurse?" How can the Beatitudes that Jesus taught be lived out in the many and varied faces of contemporary nursing? My answer came in an attempt to articulate a paradigm:

Beatitudes for Nurses

Blessed are the rural clinic nurses who minister to
the poor and the underserved,
for theirs is the kingdom of heaven.

*Blessed are the pediatric oncology nurses who mourn
for small patients lost,
for they will be comforted.*

*Blessed are the staff nurses who struggle to embrace
a wounded health care system,
for they will inherit the kingdom.*

*Blessed are the community health nurses who seek
righteousness for their marginalized clients,
for they will be satisfied.*

*Blessed are the geriatric nurses whose merciful touch
calms the anxiety of frail elders,
for they will be shown mercy.*

*Blessed are the hospice nurses whose purity of heart reflects
the single desire of midwifing the dying to new life in
Christ,
for they will see God.*

*Blessed are the maternal-child nurses who help vulnerable
mothers achieve peace in their desire to promote the
sacredness of human life,
for they will be called children of God.*

*Blessed are the missionary nurses who risk persecution and
death in the service of the oppressed,
for theirs is the kingdom of God.*

*Blessed are the military nurses who brave the ravages of
war to heal in the name of Jesus,
for great will be their reward in heaven.*

As reflected in the nursing beatitudes, there are many
avenues a nurse may tread in order to give *a cup of water* to
one who thirsts. Each of the numerous and varied acts of
serving, if done in Jesus' name, is derived from the gospel
imperative. Each occasion of care and compassion constitutes
a nurse's ministry.

CHAPTER 2.
"IN EARTHEN VESSELS":

The Nurse as Minister

*We hold this treasure in earthen vessels, that the
surpassing power may be of God and not from us.*
—2 Corinthians 4:7

I love the *earthen vessels* scripture. I think it's because I
have always been a timid soul, ever questioning my own abilities. I used to be terrified to admit that fact. What would
people think? Would such a confession indicate a poor self-
concept? Inadequate self-esteem? Although it's taken a while,
I have learned to befriend my inadequacies, my *earthen vesselness*. For I now realize, with joy and with gratitude and with
no small sense of awe, that when I am able to accomplish
something, when I am able to accomplish anything, it is not
of myself but only because of the *treasure* I hold within.

I had a wonderful learning experience about *treasure* and
earthen vesselness when I began my internship in hospital chaplaincy. As I was preparing for a ten-week summer program in

clinical pastoral education (CPE) I was struck with a panic attack. I had gone to a local Christian bookstore and purchased everything I could find on ministry to the sick and the role of the hospital chaplain. Reading did little to allay my anxiety. The dramatic reports of patient needs and the creative ministries carried out by seasoned chaplains only served to heighten my insecurity. In desperation I called a spiritual mentor, a Franciscan priest, and admitted my fears about beginning the CPE program. I said, "I've been going into patients' hospital rooms for years, first as a clinical nurse providing care and later as a nurse researcher seeking information. I feel very comfortable in both of those roles. But to walk into a patient's room and say, 'I'm your chaplain'—isn't that dreadfully arrogant?" Without missing a beat my mentor replied, "Mary Elizabeth, what's dreadfully arrogant is to think that God can't use *even you* to do his work." He chuckled and added gently: "Just try to stay out of his way!" What a wonderful response! I think it was the most important thing anyone said to me regarding the pastoral care experience. It made me think not only about my arrogance (and I really had never considered myself arrogant), but about my need for control as well. Saint Paul, who is reputed to have been the most human of men, must have known about things like arrogance and control. That's why he so beautifully reminded us that the *treasure*, the source of love and care we hold within our fragile *earthen vessels*, is indeed of God, and it is to be trusted precisely because that is so.

I have learned about *earthen vesselness* from my students also. One day during a course I teach on spirituality and nursing we were discussing the *earthen vessels* scripture, and I told the students that I imagined myself as an "earthenware jar with a lot of cracks"—cracks that have scarred the vessel over the years. My perception was that these scars were probably not a very attractive sight in the eyes of God. In response, one of my nurse-practitioner students observed, "Well, with all those cracks, just think how much better Christ's light will be able to shine through your earthen vessel." What a magnificent gift students are to those of us who teach!

The Nurse as Minister

While engaged in research on nurses caring for persons with life-threatening illnesses, I received a note from an exquisitely sensitive study participant, which read in part: *"To be a caregiver is to be called to a tender ministry. Sometimes, as we tend to the sick, especially the terminally ill, what we are witnessing is not so much the death of a mortal being...as it is the birth of an angel."*[1]

Is it appropriate to label the nurse a minister? I had pondered that question for some time. Seeking an answer, I conducted a qualitative exploration of spirituality among sixty-six contemporary practitioners of nursing. While the nurses interviewed did not identify themselves formally as ministers, they reported magnificent stories of spiritual care provided to patients and families. The data from the study led me to describe nurses as *anonymous ministers.*[2] Some nurses also shared their understanding that nursing itself was a ministry; one such was Paula, a doctorally prepared nurse-administrator with over twenty years of clinical experience, who explained her perception of the lived reality of nursing as ministry:

> Ministry is not a discreet function, a separate task. It is embedded in the careful giving of the meds, the wiping of the brow, the asking of the right questions, the acknowledgement of the patients' humanness and what they are experiencing in their sickness. I can be there to be a person of the love of God. You want to alleviate suffering, convey hope, bring love. It is in giving your care in a caring way.
>
> It is in our nursing that we recognize the spiritual side of ourselves and others."[3]

For the follower of Jesus, ministry is a vocation guided by gospel values. Christian ministry is defined as "service of the kingdom of God that flows from the call and empowerment of the Holy Spirit...(and)...involve(s) living out the call to service in the pattern of Christ's death and resurrection."[4] In a poetic vein, spiritual writer Joyce Rupp explains that all of us "are called to be instruments though which the melody of God takes shape."[5]

The comments of Sheila, a pediatric oncology nurse, reflect Joyce Rupp's analogy:

> I wanted to do nursing to be God's instrument, to let his love flow through me. I knew there was a ministry there for me. I kept saying, "This is my mission." I think people really express spiritual needs when they deal with serious illness; that's how they open up to our nursing ministry.

Sheila spoke specifically to her role as Christian minister: "For my own spiritual support I love to go back and read Mother Teresa. I think, like she says, you have to show people the love of Jesus. I don't do that all the time," Sheila admitted, "but I try."

In interviewing nurses for the spirituality study I discovered that at first most were shy about reporting instances of spiritual ministry. In more than a few cases nurse respondents began our discussions with a disclaimer to the effect that, while they were willing to speak with me about spirituality, they were not sure how much they really had to share. As I questioned them on the topic, however, examples of spiritual ministry emerged. The nurses spoke of praying with and for patients, of listening to their pain, of embracing their sufferings. At the end of the interview sessions a number of nurses reflected on their initial shyness in discussing spiritual issues. As one gerontological nurse-practitioner put it:

> I didn't think I would have a lot to talk about but I realize now that I do ministry, do spiritual care a lot; that's the best part of my nursing. But you know we don't chart it; we don't say it at report. It's just part of being a nurse, being a minister. It's the blessed part.

I believe that one of the most powerful attributes of nursing ministry is the sometimes *anonymous* nature of the ministerial activities. Whether a nurse is involved in praying with, listening to or just being present to support a patient, her actions done in the name of Christ constitute ministry. Yet the work of ministry is often hidden: carried out in the privacy of nursing a patient in a single room; standing beside a gurney in the pre-op holding area; or sitting with a homeless person in an outpatient clinic. The nurse is simply doing her job. The nurse is also, however, an *earthen vessel* holding a *treasure* within. It is in the nurse's presence that the treasure of God's love is able to be physically manifested.

The Ministry of Presence

Theological and spiritual writers speak at length about the concept of *presence:* God's presence in our lives; being present to the inspirations of the Holy Spirit; the presence of Jesus in his church; bringing a Christian presence to one's social and professional groups; and being present to those in need in terms of a preferential option for the poor. With the almost stark functionality of some of today's health care facilities and services, being truly present to the ill and the infirm poses a significant challenge. It can be extremely difficult for a nurse to find the time to exercise the kind of *presence* that might seem optimal in terms of ministry, that is, sitting and listening to or talking with patients. Practicing nurses may find themselves struggling to identify spiritual care options within a limited array of choices.

For myself—and I think it's the same for many nurses—the practice of simply being present can be one of the most emotionally challenging caring activities to accomplish. Nurses are notorious for having a goal-oriented, get-the-task-done approach. We've had to have such a mentality to make it through the day in coping with understaffed hospitals, overbooked clinics and nonscheduled emergencies. Sometimes just being present with someone can make us feel a little useless.

One day several years ago I received an early-morning call from the aunt of a seriously ill young man who was participating in my current nursing research. She said: "I'm so worried. Luke has gone to the hospital for more tests; he's really not feeling well, and I can't be with him today. He

told me he's OK and not to call you but I'm still worried."
I tried to assure Luke's aunt, and myself, that he would be
fine. He was just having some diagnostic tests, after all, and
we could see him later. I had a very busy day scheduled,
with many urgent tasks to accomplish. But somehow I
couldn't seem to get the morning started. I kept thinking
about Henri Nouwen's conceptualization of the continual
tug-of-war between the *urgent* and the *important* in our
lives.[6] I decided after a mighty struggle that while it might
not be urgent, it was important for me to be at the hospital
with Luke, with whom I had developed a close and caring
relationship. Several weeks earlier he had admitted to a
nagging fear of being alone when the time of his death
arrived. Of course, I reassured myself, that was certainly
not a worry at this point in his illness.

When I arrived at the hospital I learned that I would not
be able to spend much time with Luke, because he was
undergoing a battery of diagnostic and therapeutic procedures. He was also being transferred to the intensive care
unit. I settled into a quiet corner in the ICU waiting room
so that each time Luke was transported for a procedure I
would be able to snatch a quick visit. At our last encounter
in the ICU I held his hand and said: "I'm here." Several
times Luke told me I should go home; the nurses told me I
should go home; and, finally, after about six hours, the
ICU physician told me I should go home. Luke, he assured
me, would be in intensive care for about three weeks, and
there would be lots of time to visit in the coming days. Fifteen minutes later, without warning, Luke's vital signs bot-
tomed out; all efforts at resuscitation failed. God's time is
not our time. I thanked God with all my heart for Henri
Nouwen's teaching about the need to weigh the important
versus the urgent in prioritizing our activities. We as
earthen vessels are not always present to the *important* occasions in our lives. The light of Christ, the *treasure* within,
however, provides the direction if we can be open to the
grace of the moment.

Earthen Vessels

"Know That I Am God"

Brother Roger of Taize observed that two thousand years ago a witness to Christ wrote: "It is in vessels of Clay that we carry this treasure, the Risen Lord...to make it quite clear that the radiance comes from God and not from us."[7] It is that radiance which gives life to our ministry as nurses.

The term *vessel,* in biblical parlance, was used to designate "a wide variety of containers and instruments...the most common vessels were *earthenware.*"[8] In a New American Bible commentary on the Second Epistle to the Corinthians (4:7) it is noted that the *treasure* of which Paul preaches, God's transforming power, is envisioned as carried within earthen vessels analogous to "small terracotta lamps in which light is carried."[9] It has been speculated that if Paul was picturing a Roman procession, "earthenware pots [may have been] deliberately chosen as a foil to the magnificent treasures inside."[10] Saint Paul focused on the "theme of [our] own weakness" so that God's power in ministry would be manifest.[11] The treasure of apostolic ministry is contained within fragile vessels "so that it may be recognized that the transcendent power belongs to God."[12] Ultimately it is suggested that Paul employed the earthen vessel metaphor because he feared that "the privileges which a Christian enjoys might move him to pride."[13] Paul wanted to be certain that his audience would understand the treasure as gift, freely given by God, and never take it for granted.

Nurses who minister to the sick have little difficulty with Paul's analogy of ourselves as vessels of clay—as fragile earthenware jars ready to crack or shatter if dropped, figuratively, on too hard a surface. What may sometimes be forgotten or lacking our attention is the presence of the *treasure* we hold within. Cultivating an awareness of that treasure is an important dimension of the Christian nurse's ministry. Anne Marie, a clinic nurse who had worked for over five years with homeless clients, described how she attempted to be attentive to the presence of Christ within:

There are times I need to go someplace quiet; to be present to Christ within me. I hear God very powerfully when I have time off and get away from things and just find a quiet space. Sometimes I like to go into a chapel. In the presence of the blessed sacrament I feel God's presence in me. I just sit there in his presence. God is in my inner being. If I have time for the quietness, I know I will hear him.

When it is all chaotic at work, I know that his presence is there with me, in the chaotic moments. That helps me stay in control of the situation—knowing that his presence is there within me.

Anne Marie's desire for quiet places and times to sit in God's presence touched a chord in my own spirit. I'm afraid that I can at times be something of an activist when it comes to prayer. My goal-oriented mentality leads me to praying for and about things and people. Surely praying for needs, our own and those of others, is not a bad thing, as long as one is not seeking instant gratification, which, I have to confess, I do like. Patience is not my best virtue.

This morning at Mass our celebrant spoke about cultivating the virtue of patience, particularly in regard to prayer requests. He advised: "God is not deaf; he hears our prayers." I couldn't help but smile; they say that happens when you're guilty. Lately it seems that there have been a lot of concerns to pray about, and I began to visualize God saying: "Be at peace, Mary Elizabeth. I heard you the first time. I know exactly what you need and when you need it. My timing is perfect. Couldn't you try to trust me a little more?"

Despite my sometimes-activist prayer mentality, I know from experience that it is precisely during those precious times—when I am able to *be still and know that God is God*— that I hear his voice, that I listen to the whispering of the Holy Spirit. For the Spirit comes in quiet and in rest—in those times when we can, even if only briefly, put our concerns in his hands and simply be still. At the opening of a week-long retreat I once attended, the director advised that during the experience the participants attempt to allow their cares and anxieties to settle as the sediment in certain liquid medicines settles to the bottom of a bottle. His analogy was that as we allowed our concerns to settle, our spirits would become as transparent as the liquid and we would be able to see clearly, our vision unclouded by the muddy waters of worry and stress. This is an important image for nurses who, as earthen vessels, require clarity of vision to perceive our patients' spiritual needs as well as our own. This clarity of sight can help us to become conscious of our patients' spiritual gifts as well as their concerns.

In nursing we see splendid examples of God's radiance reflected in the *earthen vesselness* of some of our patients, who, though possessed of powerfully loving hearts, are forced to reside in the most fragile of physical bodies. One of my best teachers was Nikki, a sixteen-year-old with advanced systemic lupus erythematosus. Nikki had a brave and caring heart. She never complained about her pain because she knew her parents were so afraid. She never complained about her fears, even when she lay awake long hours at night, because she knew the nurses were so busy. She never asked why this illness had happened to her because she knew the love of her Lord. And she carried within her frail body a *treasure*.

I was head nurse on Nikki's unit during her final hospitalization and stood in awe of her sense of acceptance and equanimity. She never asked for anything…until the day one of the staff nurses came to my office with an anxious and somewhat puzzled frown. She said: "Nikki is asking for you and she doesn't look good. She says she wants to go home. She's never asked to go home before." I literally flew down the hall to Nikki's bedside; I knew it must at last truly be time for her to go *home*. She smiled weakly and said: "Will you ask Our Lady to take me home, Sister?" We prayed together to Jesus' mother; that was the first time I had ever prayed for anyone to die. My hands were trembling but I took heart from my courageous young role model. Within only a few hours Nikki did indeed go home to God. She had taught us well about the *treasure* in an *earthen vessel*. More nurses' tears!

All Who Are Sick

Jesus went about preaching the gospel and *"curing every disease and illness among the people: his fame spread to all of Syria, and they brought to him all who were sick with varying diseases...and he cured them"* (Matthew 4:23–24). Throughout his public ministry Jesus modeled the social gospel of service to those in need. He was a theorist of caring service, yet he was also a practitioner. The important thing about Jesus' ministry, the scripture suggests, is that "his words, like his healing touch, [had] the power to transform lives."[14] Matthew wrote that they brought to him *all who were sick* and *he cured them*. In commenting on the passage, Daniel Harrington notes that "the outward movement of Jesus' reputation as a teacher and healer result[ed] in the movement of many people toward him."[15] Imagine what a great number of those who were ill that must have come to Jesus on any given day, especially in a era when there were no physician's offices, walk-in clinics or emergency departments. I wonder if Jesus got very tired (we know that he sometimes went away to rest and pray), or frustrated, or even "burned-out" from all that curing? I wonder if even the grateful responses of those he healed sometimes exhausted him? I wonder if Jesus ever said to his close friends, the apostles, "I'm so tired! I've been preaching and curing people and listening to their problems for twelve days straight without a day off. I need to rest."

When I entertain thoughts like this I begin to get a little nervous; I get even more anxious when I put them on paper. Jesus, who became the Christ, the Son of the Living God, is the source of my strength and the center of my life; he is my heart. And I worry that posing such mundane questions about Jesus might seem to indicate a lack of understanding or reverence for the divinity of Christ. Yet we must remember, in thinking of Jesus, especially in thinking of Jesus as teacher and role model for nurses, that while indeed he was fully divine, he was also fully human. That is the mystery of the incarnation. One evening in a lecture on Christology the professor warned our class: "If you do not truly accept the humanity of Jesus and recognize the abandonment he experienced in his passion and death, you will never be able to comprehend the glory of the resurrection."

Curtis, a long-term survivor of HIV infection, expressed a related sentiment in discussing his personal spirituality:

> What's so important about the incarnation for us is that Jesus was human too. He really experienced the things we experience now. He knew what it's like to live, just like us. He knew what it's like to die, just like us. And so we'll know what it's like to continue existing as a spirit. So, if you have HIV, you can still preach hope, preach faith, preach unity with God. As people of the church we have learned to trust in that.[16]

Because Jesus was fully human, he understood the pain and the suffering of those who were sick; he felt sympathy for their desire to be cured. In the same way he also understands the stresses experienced by those who nurse the ill and infirm; he experienced the fatigue, both physical and emotional, that caregiving can engender. Jesus understood the human needs of the caregiver; yet he modeled for us an extraordinary message of committed service.

There Is a Blessing

Kathleen, a nurse-clinician who had worked for over fifteen years with critically ill patients, described her nursing as a *blessing:*

> There is holiness in this work; *there is a blessing* in this work. It's caring for people, ministering to people at their most fragile, at their most vulnerable times. The ICU can be very scary, and the patients depend on you. They depend on what you do, on your hands. And giving that care, it's a *blessing*. It's like the prayer of St. Teresa—we touch with the hands of Christ; we see with the eyes of Christ. There is definitely a blessing in this work of nursing the sick.

The word *blessing* is generally used by those who wish to attach a spiritual significance to a person or an occurrence. A beautiful child, a beloved parent or a caring friend may be described as a blessing in one's life. A sunny day for an outdoor event can be called a blessing on the activity. The regaining of health after an illness is often spoken of as a blessing from God. The theological understanding of the term *blessing* is related to "the authoritative pronouncement of God's favor."[17] The concept of God's blessing is often identified in the Old Testament with the story of Abraham and Isaac. In response to Abraham's great act of faith, reflected in his willingness to sacrifice Isaac, the son he loved, God said, "I swear by myself that because you acted as you did in not withholding from me your beloved son, I will *bless* you abundantly" (Genesis 22:16–17 emphasis added). In the New Testament the concept of blessing is associated with Jesus and the sacrament of the Eucharist. As Paul wrote to the Corinthians: "The cup of blessings that we bless, is it not a participation in the blood of Christ?" (1 Corinthians 10:16).

There are many blessings for nurses in ministering to the sick. Whether the nursing activities involve direct ministry, such as praying with patients, or whether the ministry is, as suggested by Paula, *embedded* in the carrying out of physical care activities with love and compassion, blessings abound. The prayer of St. Francis comes alive for the ministering nurse: "...for it is in giving that we receive." Francis of Assisi is a great role model for nurses in that he had to overcome a strong human antipathy to the disease of leprosy in order to embrace the person of the leper. As soon as Francis was able to look past the ravages of the illness and see Jesus in the victims of the disease he rejoiced in giving them care. The ministry Francis had previously viewed with great fear he came to perceive as a blessing from God.

Some military nurse corps members with whom I spoke admitted to anxiety prior to undertaking foreign assignments, especially during periods of conflict. Yet virtually all described combat field nursing as encompassing giftedness for the caregivers. A member of the United States Army Nurse Corps spoke of the blessing she had received in caring for an injured soldier in Vietnam:

> Sometimes you had experiences that you could really call a blessing—the very high points, the overtly religious. I remember a young soldier I took care of. He had been shot in the stomach. As he was getting ready to be shipped out, he reached in his pocket and pulled out a rosary, and he gave it to me. It was made of green string with just knots tied in it. He had made it himself. It was *a soldier's rosary!* I was so touched by that gift; it was a blessing between us. I still have that rosary!

Whether a nurse is providing care for a terminally ill teen, comforting a homeless person in a shelter or easing the pain of a soldier fallen in combat, caregiving done with and for and in the love of Jesus may indeed be viewed as Christian ministry. The most important thing for nurse-ministers to keep in mind is that, although in themselves they are *earthen vessels,* there is a treasure within that empowers their ministry; a power that is of Christ the Lord.

CHAPTER 3. "SOMEONE TOUCHED ME":

The Nurse as Healer

Jesus said: "Someone has touched me; for I know that power has gone out from me."
                                        —Luke 8:46

Can you think of an experience of providing care, either physical, psychological or spiritual, that left you feeling drained? This happens fairly regularly in nursing because of the intense and sensitive nature of so many of our activities. Physical care may involve nursing procedures that could be life-threatening for the patient, such as the administration of chemotherapeutic drugs or the initiation of dialytic therapy. Psychological support can have significant implications for a patient's ability to cope with a long-term chronic illness. And spiritual ministry may be the catalyst for an ill person's acceptance of a terminal diagnosis. When a nurse enters deeply into the problems or needs of a patient, she takes on her own shoulders some of the burden she is seeking to alleviate. A patient's response to a caring interaction is often a sense of lightness or relief; a nurse's response may be (as described of Jesus by the "beloved physician," Luke) the feeling that *power has gone out* from her body and her spirit.

Jesus, in his human as well as his divine nature, cared deeply for all who suffer. He was present to those in pain. He touched the sick and allowed himself to be touched. Although the woman with a twelve-year hemorrhage touched only the hem of Jesus' garment, she was nevertheless seeking healing; she was seeking to receive of Jesus' power to cure her illness. Jesus, in his compassion, felt the woman's need; he knew her pain. And in the depth of his caring Jesus experienced the feeling of *power going out* at the woman's touch. Jesus, the divine Son of God, recognized in the fullness of the humanity he so lovingly embraced, that energy may indeed go out from the minister during a healing activity.

> *And a woman afflicted with hemorrhages for twelve years, who…was unable to be cured by anyone, came up behind [Jesus] and touched the tassel on his cloak. Immediately her bleeding stopped. Jesus then asked: "Who touched me?" While all were denying it, Peter said, "Master, the crowds are pushing and pressing in upon you." But Jesus said, "Someone has touched me; for I know that power has gone out from me."*

In this scripture passage, commonly labeled "The Woman with the Hemorrhage" (Luke 8:43–48), Jesus provides a model for nurses in their roles as healers. In his ministry of healing he made himself available to a woman he did not even know, a woman who because of her hemorrhage was "ceremonially defiled."[1] Jesus was willing to be touched by the ailing woman, both physically and emotionally, in order for healing to take place. And he revealed that the interaction had impacted his spirit when he admitted, *"I know that power has gone out from me."* Commentaries on this healing passage of St. Luke's gospel emphasize the human dimension of Jesus' healing activities. As Kodell observed, "The woman with the hemorrhage touches the tassel of Jesus' cloak and is healed in a way that is almost magical. To remove this overtone of superstition, the tradition emphasizes that Jesus' power has gone out in response to faith and the healing has been more than physical."[2] Other commentators assert: "There is no magic about Jesus' clothes. He knows the difference between the casual contact of the crowd and someone reaching out in need."[3]

Nurses must also recognize *someone reaching out in need*. We touch those for whom we care; just as importantly, perhaps, we must allow ourselves to *be touched*. We need to provide our patients with the security of knowing that they can connect with us physically, psychologically and spiritually; that they can become the recipients of our energy and our compassion as they seek healing of their pain and suffering. Like Jesus, the Christian nurse must be willing to allow *power to go out* from her in the ministry of caring for those who are ill.

Megan, a master's-prepared family nurse-practitioner, spoke about the importance of a nurse allowing herself to be touched by a patient's need:

> I have seen much more suffering than I would ever have imagined, but this has helped me think about Christ's caring and his being present to people; his allowing them to touch him. This is so important today because people are hurting so much. The main thing for a nurse is to listen and let people tell you their pain; to let their hurts touch your heart. People need to be able to lean on us as they leaned on Jesus, especially when there is no answer to their suffering.

Jesus as Healer

In his book *Jesus: A Gospel Portrait,* theologian Donald Senior asserts that "by far the most significant tribute to the power of Jesus' fame is that countless people claim him as the center of their lives, as the inspiration for their best moments."[4] Thus, for the Christian nurse the concept of Jesus as healer has powerful symbolic meaning. It is estimated that "nearly one-fifth of the Gospel text is given over to Christ's healings and to discussions prompted by these cures."[5] The evangelist Matthew describes the overall healing ministry of Jesus:

> *Jesus went around to all the towns and villages...proclaiming the gospel of the kingdom, and curing every disease and illness* [9:35]; *[Jesus] went around to all of Galilee...curing every disease and illness among the people. His fame spread to all of Syria, and they brought to him all who were sick with various diseases and racked with pain...and he cured them.* (4:23–24)

Jesus' healing ministry is also described by Luke: *"[Jesus] spoke [to the crowds] about the kingdom of God, and he healed those who needed to be cured* (9:11). And Jesus' teaching regarding the need for individuals to care for their ill or injured brothers and sisters is reflected clearly in the parable of the Good Samaritan (Luke 10:30–36).

Edward Schillebeeckx observed that even in the older "proto-Christian" tradition we hear testimony from early disciples that "Jesus went about doing good," and he notes that these reports tally with "what the four gospels record about Jesus actively showing pity for the sick."[6]

We can learn much about Jesus as healer from examining gospel passages, especially those describing his miracles.[7] New Testament scholars note that much of the gospel focuses on Jesus' actions rather than his words; significant among the former are his miracles of healing the sick. Jesus' healing miracles represent not only the curing of physical illness and disease but also the restoring of spiritual health. As Rene Latourelle explains: "the bodies that Jesus cleanses, heals and restores to life are signs of the transformations of human beings into sons and daughters of the father. A miracle is a visible trace of the change effected in the human heart."[8]

Jesus' healings that have particular relevance for nurses are those included in a threefold tradition (situated close together in the scripture) described by Luke: the healing of Simon's mother-in-law (Luke 4:38–39; also Mark 1:29–30 and

Matthew 8:14–50); the cleansing of a leper (Luke 5:12–16; also Mark 1:40–45 and Matthew 8:1–14); and the healing of a paralytic (Luke 5:17–26; also Mark 2:1–12 and Matthew 9:1–8). Also relevant is John's description of the healing of a man born blind (9:1–49). These four narratives exemplify both the diversity and the breadth of Jesus' healing activity.

The Healing of Simon's Mother-in-Law

After he left the synagogue, he entered the house of Simon. Simon's mother-in-law was afflicted with a severe fever, and they interceded with him about her. He stood over her, rebuked the fever, and it left her. She got up immediately and waited on them.

Luke 4:38–39

In this healing narrative, as written by Luke, Jesus is described as curing a fever that appears to be of unknown origin; a FUO, as it is commonly called. Jesus does not need to be told a diagnosis; he has the power to cure whatever disease has invaded the woman's body, and perhaps her spirit. The cure seems to be immediate and complete, for Luke notes that, as a sign of gratitude, Simon's mother-in-law immediately arose and began to serve Jesus. The evangelist Mark adds a detail to the story in describing Jesus as employing the use of touch in the healing: "He...took her by the hand and lifted her up," which indicates a familiarity, a caring gesture; perhaps the fact of touch itself was central to the healing. Matthew also comments that Jesus touched the mother-in-law's hand. In Luke's account the concepts of touch and lifting up of Simon's mother-in-law are not specified; rather, Jesus is described as standing over the ill woman and rebuking the fever. Luke's narrative may be so written as to highlight Jesus' power. Luke is believed to have been a physician or in some way trained in the art of medicine. As a scientist, the evangelist may have thought it important to describe emphatically Jesus' mastery over illness.

This healing conveys a message for those who are sick and for their nurses. It is a reminder of the love and compassion of

God incarnate, who is concerned about the personal ills of his daughters and sons. Jesus is a model of compassionate caring for the Christian nurse.

Jesus Cleanses a Leper

> *There was a man full of leprosy in one of the towns where he was; and when he saw Jesus, he fell prostrate, pleaded with him, and said: "Lord, if you wish, you can make me clean." Jesus stretched out his hand, touched him, and said, "I do will it. Be made clean." And the leprosy left him immediately.*
> Luke 5:12–16

In Luke's narrative of the leprosy healing we see the tender and immediate response of Jesus in reaction to the faith of the leper who verbalized his trust: "You can make me clean." This healing teaches us the power of trust in God who may reward with healing of body or spirit. It also exemplifies the manner in which a request for healing should be made, in humble prostration before the Lord. The parable, finally, teaches us an important dimension of Jesus' compassion in his touching of the leper. For it was well known at the time that "to the Jews lepers were unclean, untouchable. Jesus could have healed the man with a look or a word; instead he reached out and touched him."[9]

At the end of the narrative Luke reports that Jesus "withdrew to a deserted place" to pray (4:42). This description may have been prophetic of the time to come; of Jesus' passion, when he would withdraw alone to the Garden of Gethsemane. Jesus knew that his support and comfort came from being in the presence of his Father, and he may have been gathering strength to cope with the continued demands for healing, as well as for his own forthcoming passion and death.

A difficulty for both patients and nurses, however, may occur when a desired healing or recovery does not seem to be granted even when requested with deep faith in the power of God. This narrative helps us to remember, as did the leper ("Lord, if you wish...."), that for reasons beyond our understanding, God may not choose to heal one's illness or disease at a particular time. This is when our faith is most challenged; this is when it must be kept in mind that as Christians who choose to follow a crucified Lord, we also are called upon to make a journey to Jerusalem.

The Healing of a Paralytic

> One day as Jesus was teaching...the power of the Lord was with him for healing. And some men brought on a stretcher a man who was paralyzed; they were trying to bring [him] in and set him in his presence. But not finding a way to bring him in because of the crowd, they went up on the roof and lowered him on the stretcher...in front of Jesus. When [Jesus] saw their faith...he said to the man who was paralyzed, "I say to you, rise, pick up your stretcher, and go home." He stood up immediately before them, picked up what he had been lying on, and went home, glorifying God.
>
> Luke 5:17–26

In Luke's account of the healing of the paralytic we see again the deep faith exemplified by the infirm man and his friends, who went to such great lengths to get to the feet of Jesus. It must have been painful and tiring, to say nothing of physically dangerous, for the paralyzed man and those carrying his litter to climb up on a roof, yet they did not hesitate. A strong element of trust in Jesus and his power undergirds the effort. It has been noted that this is the only occasion in the gospels where "an adult is healed because of the faith of someone else, a strong testimony to the bonds that faith forms among Jesus' followers."[10]

Luke, in distinction to evangelists Matthew and Mark, noted that Jesus' audience contained "...Pharisees and teachers of the law...who had come from every village of Galilee and Judea and Jerusalem"; Luke also asserted emphatically of Jesus: "And the power of the Lord was with him for healing."

An important lesson derived for patients and nurses from this narrative is the fact that Jesus rewarded both the faith and the extreme personal risk that those seeking the healing manifested. The paralytic and his friends requested Jesus' healing;

they demonstrated, nevertheless, that they were willing to do their part in order to accomplish the desired recovery.

It would appear that these three healing narratives of Luke have a common thread, that is, the teaching, through empirical example, of the authority and the power of Jesus. Associated with Jesus' healing activity is the importance of faith on the part of the individual seeking healing. This latter point is well demonstrated in the three scripture passages: the request for Jesus to heal Simon's mother-in-law of a condition whose etiology was unknown; the leper's trust: "If you choose, you can....."; and the deep faith demonstrated by the "roof climbers." In addition to the confidence of the one requesting healing, Luke also seems to implicitly point out that the ill person's demeanor may be important. In the first narrative, the woman with the fever immediately *rose up in gratitude and served others* after her healing; the leper *bowed low with his face to the ground* when asking for cleansing; and the paralytic risked being *dropped down* through the roof in order to be cured. In each healing the suppliant's body language, as well as his or her words, seemed to indicate both faith and humility in the face of Jesus' power and authority.

The Man Born Blind

> As he [Jesus] passed by he saw a man blind from birth. His disciples asked him: "Rabbi, who sinned, this man or his parents, that he was born blind?" Jesus answered, "Neither he nor his parents sinned; it is so that the works of God might be made visible....I am the light of the world." When he had said this, he spat on the ground and made clay with the saliva, and smeared the clay on his eyes, and said to him: "Go wash in the Pool of Siloam" (which means Sent). So he went and washed, and came back able to see."
>
> John 9:1–7

The entire ninth chapter of St. John's gospel is devoted to Jesus' healing of the man born blind. John's gospel is different from those of the other evangelists in that his readers were probably familiar with the historical facts of Jesus' life from reading the earlier gospels of Matthew, Mark and Luke. Thus, John wrote a more theological and spiritual analysis of the meaning of Jesus' life and message.

In the healing narrative of the man born blind the social milieu presents Jesus as teacher with a variety of listeners and observers. Jesus is the Rabbi performing a healing to demonstrate his power and authority. Jesus is described as the *Light of the world;* he will symbolically heal its spiritual blindness. He said: *I come into this world...so that those who do not see might see* (v. 39).

This story also demonstrates how trust in Jesus is rewarded. Jesus told the blind man to go to Siloam and wash; the man obeyed and received his sight. In believing Jesus, he affirmed his divinity. It is pointed out that while Jesus used the healing methods of his era—saliva was believed to have curative properties—the therapy "was not the important thing. What counted was the man's faith, demonstrated by his ready obedience."[11] A related theological insight is noted by Flanagan, who asserts: "He who starts out blind, takes a risk at Jesus' invitation and ends up seeing. He passes from blindness to sight, to insight. He is a striking example of the deep theology of which his cure is a sign. Jesus is indeed the light of the world."[12]

Many of us can become blind to our neighbors' needs, especially those of the poor and the infirm. In this narrative Jesus' concern about the physical as well as the spiritual blindness of one of his brothers is described. He did not blame the man or his family for the condition but acted immediately to begin healing the man's eyes and, ultimately, his spirit. This parable provides an excellent lesson for caregivers attempting to follow Jesus in today's wounded world, where both physical and spiritual healing are so desperately needed.

What then is the overall meaning of Jesus' gospel messages of healing for us as nurses? How can we interpret the scriptural narratives in light of twenty-first-century illness and disease? Theologians warn against viewing Jesus as some kind of magician engaging in spectacles that would be out of place both in his time and in ours. It is pointed out, rather, that the healings of Jesus were really "signs of salvation...signs of the Christ who alone is able to quench the hunger and thirst of this world."[13] It is also noted that Jesus did not go about seeking those who were ill: The sick and the poor came to him.[14] Donald Senior comments: "This reflects, in part, the gospel's appreciation for the active role of the sick and the disabled in seeking to be healed."[15] What Jesus really desired was that "people should believe in him, should recognize in his mission the power and the compassion of God who sent him, and should commit whatever energy and determination they had in the light of this conviction."[16] This belief in the love and compassion of God constitutes the "healing" in the era of Jesus of Nazareth as well as in our own time.

Ultimately, Christian nurses and Christian patients can take great consolation in the gospel message of Jesus' healings. Theologian Karl Rahner asserted that the Christian who is ill should have both confidence and resignation: "confidence... the will and joyous hope soon to be healthy again, because there are signs enough of this. But also resignation, accepting the sickness because we mature through it, and because even death itself is not yet the end of hope...but blessing and grace."[17]

Christ Was a Nurse

In an editorial in the *Journal of Christian Nursing,* nurse-theorist Judith Allen Shelly quotes from an address given by Florence Nightingale in which Nightingale asks her students: *"Did you ever think how Christ was a nurse, and stood by the bedside and with His own hands nursed and did for the suffering?"*[18] Florence Nightingale, a Christian, included the concept of Jesus as role model in many of her writings for the fledgling nineteenth-century community of nurses she mentored. Nightingale clearly envisioned nursing of the sick as a Christian ministry, a Christian vocational call to follow the gospel message of compassion and love for one's brothers and sisters. She wished those who followed her theory of nursing practice to care for the sick in the manner taught by Christ.

Frequently we find Jesus described, in both spiritual and medical literature, as a physician; the *divine physician*. Nurses themselves have employed this metaphor as evidenced in the title of Sister Mary Berenice Beck's early text on spirituality in nursing: *The Nurse: Handmaid of the Divine Physician*.[19] It is not usual, however, to hear of Jesus described as a *nurse*. Perhaps this simply has to do with gender. Although a number of men are currently entering the profession, nursing has from its inception been a female-dominated field. Thus one did not generally think of Jesus of Nazareth as belonging to the nursing community.

Florence Nightingale's conceptualization of Jesus as a nurse is nevertheless both important and timely. In the contemporary health care milieu, with its formalized system of managed care, the individual needs, concerns and desires of patients and families are often either ignored or only minimally attended to; recipients' wishes may be subsumed within the larger financial and sociological constraints of the care-providing agencies. Gentle *hands-on* caring, caring from the heart, by a nurse, as modeled in the life and teachings of Jesus of Nazareth, is needed more now than perhaps at any time in the history of health care.

A Listening Heart

In order to nurse as Jesus nursed, in order to heal from the heart, we need to listen with the heart. The act of listening to a patient or a family member in need is something that nurses, by nature, do well. It is part of the caring ethic of our profession. The art lies in listening with the heart as well as with the ears. Did you ever get the feeling that someone, especially a significant someone, was listening and yet not really hearing what you were trying to say? Your listener's heart was not attuned to your heart, thus the desired communication could not take place. The ability to listen with the heart is a gift for the listener as well as for the one being listened to.

God listens to us with his heart; He loves so completely that it cannot be otherwise. The prophet Jeremiah quotes the Lord as saying to his people: *"When you call me, when you go to pray to me, I will listen to you"* (Jeremiah 29:12). And Jesus himself encourages the disciples to seek God's assistance with confidence: "Ask and it shall be given to you; seek and you will find; knock and the door will be opened to you. For everyone who asks receives; and the one who seeks finds; and to the one who knocks the door will be opened" (Matthew 7:7–8). Jesus continued his teaching about the efficacy of confident prayer by explaining that the heavenly Father listens to us as a human father "cares for his children and gives them good gifts when they ask."[20] Jesus affirmed that the Father listens with his heart when he taught: *"It was not you who chose me, but I who chose you and appointed you to go and bear fruit that will remain, so that whatsoever you ask the Father in my name he may give you"* (John 15:16). Jesus finished His message with words that teach us to listen as his Father does when he admonished: *"This I command you; love one another"* (John 15:17).

The lead article in the January 1998 issue of the *American Journal of Nursing,* entitled "Recognizing and Responding to Spiritual Distress," speaks of the importance of *listening* both in terms of assessment of patients' spiritual needs: "Listen for verbal cues regarding spiritual/religious orientation....listen for significant comments, e.g., 'It's all in God's hands now'"; and intervention: "Listen actively (and) use therapeutic communication."[21] Shelly and Fish believe that listening is an "acquired skill....It involves hearing and understanding not only all of what people are saying but also what they are afraid to say."[22] This concept is supported by Brother Roger of Taize, who asserts that all who love Christ receive the pastoral gift of listening: "...listening to what hurts people about themselves. It means trying to understand what is underneath the other person's heart, until they can perceive the hope of God...even in soil that has been harrowed by tribulation."[23] In scripture the heart is described as representing the whole person in that within it, the human being meets God's word: "...it is the location where conversion takes place."[24]

To listen with your heart is to love another person. "What is the heart?" questions Henri Nouwen in the journal of his experiences at the L'Arche community Daybreak in Ontario, Canada: "It is a place of trust," Nouwen responds, "...a trust that can be called faith, hope, or love, depending on how it is being manifested....It is not so much the ability to think, to reflect, to plan or to produce that makes us different from the rest of creation, but the ability to trust. It is the heart that makes us truly human."[25] Henri Nouwen's thoughts are echoed by Sister Annice Callahan, who observed: "The heart symbolizes the center or core of the human person. It is...the place where we accept or reject the mystery of ourselves, human existence and God. The heart is sacred space. There we get in touch with the truth of our being and are open to the presence of God in our lives."[26] Ultimately, Franciscan psychologist Sister Fran Ferder asserts, true listening with the heart requires a "conscious choice": "At the heart of total listening is a clear decision to sharpen our focus both toward self and others. It means embarking on a journey *past the ears to the heart*, beyond hearing to understanding."[27]

In the midst of a busy day, especially a day of frenzied nursing tasks, the art of listening with one's heart may seem either a physical or an emotional impossibility, or perhaps both. In the hospital setting, especially, there is generally no "heart listening" time included on the daily assignment sheet. "If only there were more hours in the day..."; we say it all the time. Sometimes when I wish for more hours, more minutes, to allow my heart to listen, I think of a wonderfully caring Navy nurse I once served with. She was nursing director during my brief but treasured time in the United States Navy Nurse Corps Reserve. One day I asked the director, a nurse corps captain, how she coped with stress of running the nursing department at a large naval medical center. From observation it seemed that she never had a free minute at the hospital and was often on call when she went home. And yet, she was a great "listener with the heart" to both patients and staff.

The captain's way of managing her nursing ministry of listening, she told me, was to try and incorporate small spiritual respites into each day. She did this while driving to and from work, when walking from one building to another or even while waiting for a meeting to start. During these brief yet prayerful times, she said, "I try to imagine myself to be away on retreat." The captain derived much peace of spirit from the practice; this, I believe, was the secret of her ability to maintain a *listening heart* and, ultimately, a healing heart.

Touching with Love

As with listening, touching is natural to nurses. In the giving of nursing care we touch both physically and emotionally in situations where barriers of age or gender or even lack of acquaintance are easily surmounted. When a patient is suffering, whether physically, psychologically or spiritually, the gentle touch of a nurse's hand is rarely rebuffed; a tender word of comfort is rarely ignored. Loving touch is natural; it's expected; it's what we do as members of a healing profession. The act of touching another with care, touching another with love, contains within it the properties of healing and of cure.

Nurse historian Josephine Dolan reminds us that Jesus modeled for nurses the fact that we were to touch. She pointed out that Jesus did not just stand at a distance from those who were ill but physically touched them, allowed them to feel his loving hands, in the process of healing their ills: "Christ gave individual attention to the needs of all by touching, anointing and taking the hand."[28] A poignant example is Jesus' care for the young daughter of Jairus. The synagogue leader told Jesus that his daughter was at the point of death and begged him: "Please, come lay your hands on her that she may get well and live" (Mark 5:23). Jesus immediately left a crowd of disciples and went with

Jairus to the room where his daughter lay ill: *"He took the child by the hand and said to her* 'Talitha koum,' *which means: 'Little girl, I say to you, arise!' The girl, a child of twelve, arose immediately and walked around"* (Mark 5:41–42). We as nurses may not be able to heal a physical problem but the giving of a caring, loving touch, as exemplified by Jesus, may go far in healing the emotional suffering accompanying a serious illness.

As a member of the L'Arche community in Ontario, Canada, Henri Nouwen practiced loving touch in his interactions with Adam, a severely handicapped young adult. For some time Father Nouwen provided morning care, including bathing, feeding and dressing Adam; he likened the experience to caring for Jesus:

> I have heard about and read about the life of Jesus, but I was never able to touch or see him. I was able to touch Adam. I saw him and I touched his life....And what is said of Jesus must be said of Adam: "Everyone who touched him was healed" (Mark 6:56). Each of us who touched Adam has been made whole somehow.[29]

A group of patients who taught me a lot about loving touch were frail elders residing in a nursing home. During a two-year case study of the home[30] I spent many hours visiting with the residents. Almost invariably the elders would reach out and take my hand during a visit; sometimes they would hold it up to their faces, as my mother used to do when I was a child. With the decrease in functional abilities, both physical and cognitive, a heightened sensitivity to touching and to being touched often develops. Elders recognize the brevity of life and are willing to live and to love in the moment. They have time to touch and to be touched, to be totally present to another. Elders know they must not live in the future, for the future is now. This is an important lesson for all of us. I developed treasured relationships with these frail elders and experienced the healing power of both giving and receiving loving touch on many occasions.

Holy Hands

In the carrying out of *loving and healing touch,* nurses need to have *holy hands.* But what does this concept indicate in terms of contemporary professional nursing practice? What do *holy hands* mean for the nurse as healer? Henri Nouwen wrote of his concern about the increased sophistication of the healing professions, which he believed was leading to depersonalized care.[31] Nouwen advised that "the healer has to keep striving for a spirituality...by which the space can be created in which healer and patient can reach out to each other as fellow travelers sharing the same broken human condition."[32] Nouwen's admonition to "reach out" represents the spiritual undergirding for conceptualizing the nurse as a healer possessed of *holy hands.*

Nurses, as healers, take the place of Christ in laying holy hands on their suffering patients. The great Saint Teresa of Avila reminded us of this with the words of her well known admonition:

> *Christ has no body now on earth but yours; no hands but yours; no feet but yours. Yours are the eyes through which the compassion of Christ must look out on the world. Yours are the feet with which he is to go about doing good. Yours are the hands with which He is to bless His people.*[33]

What a blessed thought for nurses to understand that their hands may be used as Christ's hands, to care for and comfort his people. Nurse's hands are precious instruments to be employed in the art as well as the science of their profession. So often we take our hands for granted; simply seeing them as physical appendages to help us accomplish desired tasks. Yet the term *hand* is found "approximately fifteen hundred times" in scripture.[34] Edwards notes that "healing the sick is closely associated with [the word] *hand* in the New Testament, indicating the transference of spiritual and physical wholeness" in a touch (Mark 5:23; Luke 13:13).[35]

Nurses may facilitate spiritual or physical wholeness and healing through using their hands in such caring activities as bathing a patient, changing a surgical dressing, touching an elder with tenderness or hugging a frightened child. The holiness of nurses' hands is derived from the holiness of their caring, the holiness of their love, the holiness of their devotion.

"You Who Are Burdened"

Jesus told all who were burdened to "come to him" and be healed. In their roles as healers, nurses must also respond to the needs of many who are burdened and who come for comfort and support. Often patients carry burdens and fears that they entrust to nurses to aid in their healing care. At times nurses take on themselves the patients' pain and stand with them in their time of suffering. They may also become the patients' advocates, as Jesus was our advocate before the Father. Early nursing theorist Virginia Henderson wrote poignantly of such empathy in an *American Journal of Nursing* article in which she asserted that the nurse is "temporarily the consciousness of the unconscious; the love of life for the suicidal; the leg for the amputee; the eyes of the...blind; confidence for the young mother; [and] the mouthpiece for those too weak or withdrawn to speak."[36]

And yet to carry out our role as healers, to ease the burdens of our patients, nurses need to be ourselves healed. We each need to place our own burdens in a loving heart, that we may be free and unencumbered to provide loving care for others. I have learned, after many years of being a "Martha" (and I speak more about this in a later chapter), that valuing the "Mary" side of my self is critical to living the gospel message of Jesus. Mary and Martha war within me constantly, but now I recognize, at least most of the time, how important it is to, like Mary, "sit at Jesus' feet." How much I need those times of quiet prayer, of quiet listening, in order to carry out my nursing activities with compassion and love.

The problem, of course, for myself as for many nurses, whether practitioners, managers, researchers or academicians, lies in finding the time and the space for quiet prayer. Trappist Father Basil Pennington, a distinguished scholar and practitioner of prayer, has written a wonderful book entitled *Lectio Divina: Renewing the Ancient Practice of Praying the Scriptures*.[37] Father Basil, although himself a monk and a student of the fathers and mothers of the desert, is acutely sensitive to the crushing schedules of daily life that burden many of us in today's society. While he advocates the need for "going apart," as did the desert fathers and mothers, to be in the presence of the Lord, Father Basil also gives practical suggestions for how this might be done in the midst of a busy day:

> *Our place apart can be a corner of our room where our Bible proclaims a Presence. Our going apart may be just turning our chair away from our desk with all its affairs, leaving the world behind for a few minutes while we rest in the Presence and know ourselves to be held in a great and tender love. Or we may find our own going apart to be found in a short walk to a church, a library, or a park, some quiet spot where we can sit for a bit in the quietness and know something of the [quiet] of the desert.*[38]

I talked about this with some of my graduate students, most of whom also hold part-time nursing jobs to help finance their education. I wanted to see if we could expand on Father Basil's suggestions for "going apart" during a busy day of nursing practice or nursing education. One of the ideas suggested was to incorporate prayer or scripture reading into trips on the Metro, our city's rapid transit system. A doctoral student, who is also a teaching assistant, admitted that she had been inspired one morning, on the way to her clinical placement, by observing a fellow passenger reading a small Bible. The student suddenly realized that she could use her own Metro trips each day for times of quiet prayer or spiritual reading. Another idea, from an emergency room nurse, was that one could practice times of prayerful listening while waiting for a treatment to be initiated or a central line to be inserted if one is attuned to the loving Presence of God in the emergency room setting.

Finally one of the students, who had done a significant amount of home care as a Visiting Nurses' Association nurse, described using the few minutes between patient visits as times of "going apart." "A few years ago," she admitted, "I used to rush out to the car for a cigarette. Now I just sit there for about three to five minutes. I pray for the patient I just saw and I ask for guidance with the next patient." Each of us as nurses will need to find his or her own time and space to "go apart," to experience, as Father Basil so eloquently puts it, being "held in a great and tender love." These moments are the heart and the strength and the source of our ability to comfort and to heal. Jesus was able to heal the woman with the hemorrhage because he was continually "held in [the] great and tender love" of his Father. He came to us, the incarnate Son of God, that we his brothers and sisters might be held in that same love. He came that love might fill us with such a spirit of compassion and tenderness that power might also go out of us in caring for the ill and the infirm. We, as nurses, are indeed blessed to be used as instruments of God's healing love.

CHAPTER 4.
THROUGH RAGING WATERS:

The Nurse's Woundedness

"When you pass through the water, I will be with you;
in the rivers you shall not drown."
                                                    —Isaiah 43:2

In the late 1980s I was engaged in nursing research with AIDS patients, many of whom died only months after I had met them; this was before the era of sophisticated therapeutic regimens. I tried to attend as many memorial services as possible. I did so for the families of my patients who had died and also for myself; I was becoming the wounded researcher. At first I kept a record of the numbers in my head. After approximately thirty services I stopped counting; it hurt too much. I remember a nurse colleague saying: "You don't have time to grieve one death before another one happens; how are you handling this?" I believe that my answer was something like, "Not very well!" I told her that I always felt sad and burdened as I drove to a memorial service; there was such grief over the loss of a young life. But I felt comforted by the close of the service; the time of remembering and praying and crying seemed to ease a little the sadness in my soul. My friend told me I should write about that. I never have; until now.

Ultimately my way of dealing with the woundedness I experienced in working with those dying of AIDS, the only way I could deal with it, was to place my hurt, my frustration, my sadness into the loving hands of Jesus, who understands suffering so much better than any of us ever could. To be a nurse is to know pain, to know woundedness, and sometimes to pass through water that may indeed be experienced as "raging water." Early in the research I was invited to give a talk on working with those in the final stages of AIDS. I spoke about my involvement with the patients and their families and about the personal suffering that followed a death. After my presentation a member of the audience came to me and said: "I've been working with AIDS patients for five years and you'll get over being so involved; if you don't you'll burn out. You need to distance yourself." I listened politely. My veteran AIDS caregiver didn't really want a response, but after she walked away I prayed silently: "Please dear God, don't let me ever 'get over' becoming involved with my patients." Being involved, being wounded, passing *through raging waters*, is what nursing is all about. Nursing isn't always easy; it doesn't always feel good. But as Christian nurses we have the blessed gift of knowing, as the prophet Isaiah so beautifully taught, that God will be with us, and that *"in the rivers"* of suffering we *"shall not drown."*

Through Raging Waters

The Problem of Suffering

For a nurse to truly be involved, to be a compassionate caregiver, an understanding of the spiritual meaning of suffering is critical. Suffering has been defined as "any experience that impinges on an individual's or a community's sense of well-being."[1] Richard Sparks observed, further, that suffering "may be physical, psychological, interpersonal or spiritual, though in most instances, it is a combination of these."[2] A related yet slightly expanded definition of suffering is that articulated by Dominican Sister Mary Ann Fatula: "...the disruption of inner human harmony caused by physical, mental, spiritual, and emotional forces experienced as isolating and threatening our very existence."[3] Fatula goes on to explain that suffering is not caused by God, "the author of all good," but is "inherent in the universe's natural process and in the uniqueness of human freedom."[4]

Generally those who are suffering or who care for those who suffer seek to alleviate the distress in whatever way possible. For persons grounded in spirituality, prayer is a usual recourse. Sometimes, as noted in chapter three, the prayers we pray seem to go unanswered, and we may question ourselves and our prayers, or perhaps even God. Are my prayers not holy enough? Have I sinned too seriously for God to listen? Is God too busy with things more important than what I'm asking for? And, in times of deep pain and anguish, we may even ask. "Does God really care?"

In discussing a Christian response to suffering, Father William Marravee asserted: "The Christian God's specialty does not lie in being able to take suffering away from us occasionally, but in accepting solidarity with all those who suffer."[5] He explains that God has, in fact, overcome suffering by taking it upon himself and sharing it with us. God has demonstrated this sharing by making "the suffering and death of his Jesus the expression of his love for us."[6]

All suffering involves mystery. We do not understand the reason for it. We struggle with the question "Why?" Accepting the concept of mystery is a very difficult task for contemporary persons, barraged as we are with media reports of scientific breakthroughs. We balk at the idea of being unable to make sense of an occurrence. We delight in mystery as entertainment in books, films and plays, because always at the end we can trust that the mystery will be solved, that we shall have our *aha* moment. We will not be left wondering. But such is not the case with the divine mystery of Jesus' passion, the holy mystery that only faith can help us to accept in this life. As theologian Dom Hubert van Zeller has observed: "The Passion is described as the mystery of Christ's suffering. It was a mystery at the time because people could not reconcile it with what they had expected. In the sense that we can never fully understand the idea of God's suffering, the Passion is still a mystery."[7] Van Zeller goes on to explain that if our sufferings are somehow to "fit into the Passion of Christ," there will be mystery about them as well, and they will "make demands upon our faith."[8] Suffering is not something one usually seeks, but it can provide a wonderful opportunity for growing more deeply in Christ. "The value of the occasion of sickness, if it will exist," wrote Feider, "is placed on it by the [ill] person or friends of the [ill] person who accept it, who surrender with openness to...the wider possibilities of God's plan."[9]

As Christians and as Christian nurses, we are called upon not to choose suffering but to accept it. Theologian Patrick Reilly asserts: "Gethsemane revealed the striking simplicity of the Christian attitude toward pain. If pain can be avoided, avoid it, 'let this chalice pass'; there is to be no masochistic traffic with anguish. But, if pain cannot be avoided, 'Thy will, not mine,' then it must not only be borne but made fruitful."[10] Positive coping with suffering, for a Christian, can provide a deep sense of peace and freedom if dealt with from a spiritual foundation. Sister Rosemarie Carfagna reminds us that Christians can find courage and strength to look beyond the "immediate experience of physical or mental distress to the transcendent source of life and death, suffering and joy. They look to God and to the person of Jesus Christ."[11]

After witnessing and being empathetic toward the suffering of patients for long periods of time some nurses experience a condition that used to be called burnout, and which has more recently been labeled compassion fatigue. The symptoms may be physical or emotional and can, at times, interfere with one's practice of nursing. In discussing ways for nurses to deal with the syndrome, Carla Johnson suggests that an important coping mechanism is feeding oneself spiritually.[12] This may be done though a variety of activities, such as prayer, meditation and spiritual reading, as suggested in the previous chapter. Seeking counseling from a pastoral caregiver or spiritual friend may also prove helpful in offering an objective view of the situation, as well in providing some suggestions for remedying the fatigue. The ultimate spiritual guide to assist us in navigating the *raging waters,* however, is the strength and care of the God who will carry us when we cannot walk, who will support us when we cannot stand, who will lead us when we cannot see the way. As the prophet Isaiah powerfully taught, the Lord, who has called us by name, will calm our *raging waters* and give us his peace if we but ask.

Be Not Afraid

> But now, thus says the LORD.../Fear not, for I have redeemed you;/I have called you by name:/you are mine./When you pass through the water, I will be with you;/in the rivers you shall not drown./When you walk through fire, you shall not be burned; the flames shall not consume you./For I am the LORD your God, the Holy One of Israel, your savior.
>
> Isaiah 43:1–3

I remember once being very afraid as I was discerning a major change in my life. I called a priest friend and said: "When I prayed 'Morning Prayer' today the first psalm began: 'My heart is steadfast, O God; my heart is steadfast' [Psalm 108]. Well, my heart is steadfast; I just wish my stomach would catch up!" He laughed and replied: "That's just the good old human condition, Mary Elizabeth. Why do you think that every time we read in scripture about an angel of the Lord appearing to someone, the angel begins her message with the words: '*Fear not!*'?" My priest friend's words, and especially his laughter, were comforting. They did not completely alleviate my anxiety, but they did make me aware that I was not unique in my fearfulness.

One of my most treasured books is Hannah Hurnard's scripturally based allegory *Hinds' Feet on High Places.* I identify with the protagonist, Much Afraid, as she struggles with her fears in attempting to gain the *hinds' feet* needed for ascent to the high places where the Chief Shepherd dwells. In the allegory the Shepherd comforts Much Afraid with the promise he alone can give:

> *Even if the way up to the high places appears to be obscured and you are led to doubt whether you are following the right path, remember the promise, "Thine ears shall hear a word behind thee, saying: This is the way, walk ye in it, when ye turn to the right hand and when ye turn to the left." Always go forward along the path of obedience as far as you know it until I intervene, even if it seems to be leading you where you fear I could never mean you to go.*[13]

There are myriad issues associated with the current health care system that might make contemporary Christian nurses wonder if they are "following the right path." All one has to do is turn on the evening news to hear the positive benefits of such procedures as euthanasia and cloning touted in certain quarters of the scientific community. A nurse colleague, who is presently director of research at a large urban medical center, recently expressed her concern that the values of Christian nurses may be seriously challenged in the not-too-distant future. She fears that hospital staff nurses will be asked to assist or at least to support the conduct of procedures whose ethical boundaries they question, if they want to keep their jobs. It will be in just such situations that Christian nurses will need to, as the Shepherd advised, "go forward along the path of obedience" to their faith beliefs and values, knowing that they are following the path set out in the gospel message for those who would be followers of Jesus.

Henri Nouwen admits that we are a "fearful people," concerned with many fears related to such issues as illness, accidents and job loss.[14] Nouwen asserts, however, that despite all our fears it is possible to live in a "house of love": "the house of love is the house of Christ, the place where we can think, speak and act in the way of God; not in the way of a fear-filled world" (p. 21). What great joy and confidence the thoughts of both Henri Nouwen and Hannah Hurnard provide for nurses faced with fears, especially those fears related to challenges to their faith. Letting go of our fears, being *not afraid* is no easy task; I would not dare to suggest it to be so. But with faith it is possible. A sister friend told me that the spiritual advisor of her community had recently reminded the sisters that when they possess material things, those same things possess them in return. How true that is! We get ourselves loaded down with "stuff" and then spend endless hours taking care of the "stuff," which supposedly was obtained to make our lives easier and more pleasant. It's the same with fear. The more fear we possess, the more that fear possesses us. Sometimes we collect fears because we think them necessary in order to protect us from dangerous situations. I am surely not advocating the abolition of appropriately prudent concerns, such as fear of wild animals, fear of driving in front of a speeding train or fear of leaping off a twenty-story building (even if you are into Bungee jumping). But many fears, at least many of my fears, are really founded in lack of faith that God is truly Master of the universe, is truly the Master and center of my life. Indeed our greatest fear, our greatest reason to *be afraid,* should be the fear of not loving, the fear of not appreciating and not responding to the great and tender love that the Lord continually offers to us.

I get most afraid when I'm alone, or at least when I think that I'm alone. I recently confessed to being afraid about a particular decision to a spiritual advisor. She replied: "Well, you know that you're not doing this by yourself, don't you? God is right there with you, in the midst of it." My advisor's response made me feel like a bright light had just been turned on to warm my heart and dissipate my anxiety. It was as if I could suddenly feel the presence of God in my decision making; I could trust that my prayers were being listened to by a dear and loving Father whose only wish was to give me the greatest happiness I could possibly have: that of drawing me to himself. Brother Roger of Taize assures us that while we all experience a solitude that no human intimacy can fill, we are "never alone": "Let yourself be plumbed to the depths," he advises, "and you will see that, in your heart of hearts, in the

place where no two people are alike, Christ is waiting for you.
And what you never dared hope for springs to life."[15]

A Heartsore Refusal

Saying No with Love

One of the fears to which many people admit is the fear of
saying no. There is certainly some basis in reality for this fear.
Saying no to a person who is asking something of one puts
the individual refusing at risk of being labeled uncaring, judg-
mental, lacking in understanding or compassion, or perhaps
several other unpleasant adjectives. It is natural to wish to be
well regarded by those with whom we interact; saying no may
jeopardize a positive image of ourselves formerly held by the
person whose request was refused. The desire to be liked is
just as valid for a nurse as for any other individual. There are
many times in nursing, however, when we must say no for the
sake of a patient's well-being. There are times, for example,
when although our hearts are sore, we need to say no to:

- the pain-racked post-op patient who longs for more anal-
  gesic than would be safe for recovery;
- the critically ill child who cries feverishly for a drink of
  water yet whose small body cannot tolerate anything by
  mouth;
- the elderly nursing home resident who begs to go home,
  when in reality, there is no longer a home to go to.

Saying no to patients such as these can be one of the most
difficult of nursing activities for those who are called to care.
Being forced to say no can make one defensive or irritated at
being asked to do the impossible. Thus it becomes even more
important to be consciously loving and sensitive: to let our
patients know that, while we may not be able to respond pos-
itively to a desire, we say no with wounded hearts and a deep
sense of caring for their needs. I mentioned this idea to a
group of students in my spirituality and nursing course, and

they all validated the fact that saying no is one of the hardest things for a nurse to do.

Sometimes, probably a lot more often than we would like, God says no to us, even to those requests for things which we think would draw us closer to him. I learned about *saying no with love* when this happened to me. I had asked for something that I thought was of God, which I thought would deepen my living the gospel message of Jesus and bring me closer to his heart. The person to whom I made the request— and who was truly God's instrument in the situation— responded that while she was forced to say no, her *heart was sore* over the refusal. She sent me a beautiful and poignant letter expressing an acute awareness that her response would no doubt bring pain; she also acknowledged her trust that my life was being guided by God's great and tender love, which would ultimately reveal his will, the only thing that really matters, after all. While it is true that the letter brought the pain of disappointment, the love and caring with which the *saying no* was done did much to alleviate my hurt.

Saying no to a patient's request, especially when one would prefer to say yes, can make nurses want to pull back, to distance from the interaction for self-protection. And yet this is precisely when they need to reach out in caring and concern; to comfort the patient at the time of refusal. A nurse who has said no may also need to be prepared to accept anger and frustration from a disappointed patient. But it is in continuing to care, in the face of such a fretful response, that a nurse has the opportunity to practice the fullness of Christian love and Christian compassion in the manner taught by Jesus of Nazareth.

Embracing the Pain

Sister Macrina Wiederkehr has written that "there is nothing: no thing, no person, no experience, no thought, no joy, no *pain*, that cannot be harvested and used for nourishment on our journey to God."[16]

Pain is something with which nurses are intimately familiar; we know it on a first-name basis. We meet it in different guises and disguises every day. Sometimes the pain has a positive outcome. There is the pain of a laboring mother-to-be announcing the impending birth of a new life; there is the pain of a child's inflamed appendix signaling the need for healing surgical intervention. Very often, however, the pain is of an unwanted or feared disease or illness. In some of these cases the physiological outcome will not be positive.

One of the most painful and dreaded potential health deficits for older adults, and for many families and nurses as well, is the syndrome of senile dementia, or Alzheimer's disease. In an article commenting on his mother's seven-year experience with Alzheimer's, philosopher Richard Parry spoke about the pain of his "entanglement" with his dying mother's care. He also explained the importance of such interaction:

> I...believe that this entanglement is part of what it is to be a human being. Without it our humanity would lack an important dimension. To go to the edge of suffering with another is to be a human being. Being human does not mean to be an autonomous individual. To be human is to be entangled with one another in the most elemental ways.[17]

As nurses, providing hands-on care, we cannot avoid becoming "entangled" to some degree with our patients' pain. Anne, the head nurse of an experimental Alzheimer's unit in a large research medical center, described the pain her staff nurses suffered in their daily encounters with dementia patients. Anne gave an example:

> There is this one patient; well they're all very difficult for the staff. I mean seeing the patients deteriorate. But this patient, he's only forty-three and he has very early Alzheimer's. The thing is, he's a scientist, a biophysicist; he's really bright and he knows the score. He can see his cognitive abilities disappearing; and, of course, he's saying "why me." And every time he comes in to the unit he's failed a little more. And it's tearing the staff apart. They grieve over him and I think they identify too, because he's so young. It's hard for me to know what to say or how to comfort them.

Recently there was a beautiful and poignant column, written by His Eminence, James Cardinal Hickey, in the Washington archdiocesan Catholic newspaper. The piece was entitled, "Alzheimer's Takes a Friend Away." As I read the article, I had tears in my eyes; I thought of the scientist with early Alzheimer's and of Anne's nurses. I immediately wrote to the cardinal and asked his permission to retell the story so that I could share his comforting thoughts on the spirituality of coping with Alzheimer's disease.

His Eminence began the column by describing a visit to a dear friend, a brother priest, with whom he had interacted through innumerable visits and letters over many years. The cardinal explained:

> *But last summer he no longer knew me. When I walked into his room, I greeted him just as I had done a thousand times before. I began the usual small talk and banter, but nothing seemed to register. He smiled at me as one smiles at a stranger. All attempts to remind him of our friendship failed. Alzheimer's had taken my friend away.*[18]

His Eminence admitted that since the visit he had prayed for his friend and also for "the grace to understand and accept this mysterious form of suffering."[19] He shared his perception of the spirituality of Alzheimer's disease:

> *Alzheimer's patients eventually lose almost all their memory and their capacity to function but they retain their humanity. Though physically and mentally impaired, they are human beings possessing their full human dignity and worth. No, the brain is not immune from Alzheimer's. But Alzheimer's cannot reach the soul. Lodged deeper than one's subconscious, in the depths of the human soul, is the true content of one's life. It is there where God is met and loved. It is there where true human friendships are formed and where lasting memory of loved ones resides. In the recesses of the soul is written the true story of one's life.*[20]

Cardinal Hickey has given us, as nurses, a superb example of how to understand the suffering of a disease like

Alzheimer's; of how to embrace the pain of caring for those living with the condition. Although an Alzheimer's patient may not be able to communicate in the way we might wish, we need to be acutely aware, as His Eminence reminded us, that the patient is still a person of dignity and worth, because God dwells in his or her soul. For the person who is suffering from the dementia—the confusion, the forgetfulness, the inability to articulate thoughts clearly—there may seem a terrible loss of dignity. This then becomes the nurse's trust. In a letter to *America*, oncology nurse Sandy Focht reported that when one of her patients bemoaned the loss of dignity experienced as part of his chemotherapy treatment, she explained that "a patient's dignity is not lost; it is just entrusted to someone who cares."[21] We, as Christian nurses, must never cease to be persons who care, persons to whom a patient's dignity may be entrusted. And we need to remember always, in our tasks of caring, that a disease such as Alzheimer's can indeed *never reach the soul.*

The Nurse's Woundedness

> *When trials arise within you or misunderstandings arise from without, never forget that in the same wound where the pangs of anxiety are seething, the...[love of Christ] is also being born.*
>
> Brother Roger of Taize[22]

In the book *Spirituality and Nursing: Standing on Holy Ground,* I briefly introduced the nurse's role as a wounded healer. The concept usually evokes thoughts of Henri Nouwen's classic book *The Wounded Healer,* in which the author likens the wounded minister to the Talmudic identification of the awaited Messiah, that is, the one who never unbinds his own wounds all at once so that he shall always be available to help others in need of healing.[23] Many nurses are wounded healers. Their wounds are of varying shapes and sizes. The wounded nurse is a compassionate nurse. I remember once talking with someone who said rather irritably, "I just don't understand people who are always getting ill. I've never been sick a day in my life." I thought: "How sad!" I don't really mean I was sad that she had never been sick; that was a blessing. But I would never want that person to be my nurse; fortunately she had no attraction to a career in the health care field.

To be a compassionate nurse one can use his or her own wounds as a source of understanding and strength; the nurse may identify with the wounds of the patient. Compassion has been described as "suffering alongside" another.[24] Judy Shelly and Sharon Fish assert that "the therapeutic use of self requires that a nurse be vulnerable."[25] They explain that being compassionate, suffering alongside the patient, does, however, open the nurse to the possibility that she "too will experience pain."[26] The theme is echoed by hospice nurse Kathy Kalina in her book *Midwife for Souls,* when she admits:

> In nursing school I was taught that a good nurse keeps a professional distance so that she can effectively care for the patient and protect herself emotionally. It took me years to discover the truth; the only way to protect yourself from the pain of compassion is never to love.[27]

Margaret, a pediatric nurse-practitioner, described her understanding of being a wounded healer:

> Once when I was helping with a very painful procedure with a young child, a student nurse said to me: "How do you get to the point where this doesn't bother you?" I said: "Oh, no, you don't ever want to get to the point where it doesn't bother you. You may get more adept at how you handle your response, but you always need to feel the pain; you always need to let it bother you! That's part of being a healer; your own woundedness. If you ever get over feeling the patient's pain, then you need to get out of nursing."

Margaret explained her personal strategy for coping with such woundedness:

> When I'm dealing with a dying child, usually I'm so caught up with being there, helping them, that I don't

think about my pain. But after it's over, that's when I start to digest it; that's the way nurses usually act; we get caught up in the doing. You don't have time to think and sometimes that's bad. It hits me when I'm driving, when I'm alone. The thing that really helps me is reading scripture or spiritual things and praying with my family. We read and we pray together and that helps me a lot; the strength of the love of God and the love of Jesus.

In speaking of Jesus as the consummate wounded healer, Father Ralph DiOrio notes that, as Christ received the wounded, "...so we who would experience the crucified love would...be sent forth by [Jesus] to other wounded seekers....We are all wounded healers," Father DiOrio asserts, "especially after we have experienced his wounded love through our own wounded searchings."[28]

This chapter has been about the nurse's blessing in woundedness; the ministry of the nurse as a wounded healer. It is about the wounded nurse's ability to cope with such issues as suffering, fear, pain and the difficulty of having to say no to a patient's request. Mostly though, the chapter is about the Christian nurse's gifts in the midst of these *raging waters:* the gift of the Father's presence as source of strength and courage; the gift of the Spirit's whisperings as source of wisdom and understanding; the gift of the Son's embrace as source of compassion and love. The nurse's woundedness allows him or her to be open to receive these gifts and to share them with others. Ultimately, then, the woundedness itself is a gift—a gift to be accepted, a gift to be understood, a gift to be treasured. To be wounded is to be human; to be wounded is to be vulnerable; to be wounded is to be a reflection of the consummate wounded healer, Jesus of Nazareth, the touchstone of our hope and the center of our lives.

CHAPTER 5.
WITH EAGLES' WINGS:

The Nurse's Strength

---

*They that hope in the LORD will renew their strength,
they will soar as with eagles' wings.*
                                                    —Isaiah 40:31

The previous chapter focused on the nurse's woundedness—on the blessing and gift that the nurse's own woundedness may become in supporting his or her role as a wounded healer. Henri Nouwen's analogy of the Talmudic wounded healer, prefigure of the Messiah, was described to explain the importance of a healer never unbinding his or her wounds all at once in order to be available to assist others. Certain old wounds, however, no longer need to be bound; they have healed over with well-worn scars. And in looking carefully at those scars one finds significant new life and health in the regenerated tissue. Those who have been wounded and have treated their scars with the healing balm of hope in the Lord will indeed have renewed energy:

Those who "hope in the LORD will renew their strength,/ they will soar as with eagles' wings." "They will run and not grow weary,/walk and not grow faint." (Isaiah 40:31)

Some days our energy seems drained. We feel that if we tried to run we would grow very weary; if we tried to walk any distance we really might faint. While these feelings could be the result of a physical problem that needs attention, they can also be related to our state of mind. And it is in the latter case that *"hope in the Lord"* will be the correct and, in fact, the only remedy to renew our strength and give us the ability to *"soar as with eagles' wings."*

Eagles' Wings

The Gift of Hope

When the prophet Isaiah wrote that one might soar *"as with eagles' wings,"* he identified the criterion for achieving that characteristic as the individual possessing *hope in the Lord.* A nurse friend told me once that while the Irish (she's also Irish) are very good in terms of the virtues of faith and love, they don't do so well in the hope department. I think she was trying to give me a not-so-subtle message. Although I don't like to admit it I've always been a worrier; rather than hoping for the best, I can always conjure up some fear about the potential for the worst. I'm embarrassed to admit this because it validates my friend's opinion. It also makes me face my lack of trust and confidence in the God who has cared so lovingly for me for so many years. I sometimes wonder if God must be thinking, "How much more will it take, Mary Elizabeth, before you know that I love you?"

Hope is a wonderful virtue and a wonderful gift. In writing his letter to Titus the apostle Paul emphasized the importance of hope when he spoke of the incarnation: *"For the grace of God has appeared, saving all and training us to...live...devoutly in this age, as we await the blessed hope, the appearance of the glory of the great God and of our savior Jesus Christ"* Titus 2:11–13.

Hope is an important characteristic for nurses, because there may well be times that our patients need to borrow some of our hope when their own optimism is compromised by illness or disease. The word *hope* usually makes us think of the anticipation that something good or desirable will occur. Hope is defined theologically by Monika Hellwig as focusing our "attention, affectivity, and commitment to action toward the future goal of fulfillment in God."[1] In their new book *Called to Care: A Christian Theology of Nursing*, Judith Shelly and Arlene Miller assert that "hope has always been a vital aspect of nursing, for both nurses and their patients. The hopeful nurse," they add, "finds strength to continue working in the face of great odds."[2]

For the Christian nurse hope is centered in the incarnation—in the splendidly hopeful example of Jesus' passion and resurrection. When we meet Jesus in the gospel and consider the many painful experiences he encountered in his humanity, hope truly becomes a living virtue. Our greatest hope is in the resurrection of Jesus of Nazareth who became *the Christ*. In the "Office of Readings" from the *Liturgy of the Hours* for Monday of Holy Week, a sermon given by Saint Augustine is read in which he asserts that "the passion of our Lord and Savior Jesus Christ is the *hope* of glory [emphasis added]."[3] Augustine explains: "The death of the Lord our God should not be a cause of shame for us; rather it should be our greatest hope, our greatest glory. In taking upon himself the death that he found in us, he has most faithfully promised to give us life in him, such as we cannot have in ourselves."[4]

My favorite evangelist is St. Luke; I suppose that's because of his identification as the *beloved physician*. The early portion of St. Luke's gospel, beginning with chapter four, "The Ministry in Galilee," describes Jesus' life in essentially hopeful terms. In the ministry of Galilee Jesus had many followers and there were multiple healings of illness and disease such as "The Cure of the Demoniac" (Luke 4:31–37), "The Cure of Simon's Mother-in-Law" (Luke 4:38–39), "The Cleansing of a Leper" (Luke 5:12–16) and

"The Healing of a Paralytic" (Luke 5:17–26). However, early on Jesus was rejected in his own land of Nazareth: *"They rose up, drove him out of the town, and led him to the brow of the hill on which their town had been built, to hurl him down headlong"* (Luke 4:29). Nevertheless, when Jesus called Simon and the other apostles they left everything and followed him (Luke 5:11). Jesus continued to go about his public life carrying out the caring activities of pardoning sin (Luke 8:36); raising the dead (Luke 7:11); and teaching in parables, for example, "The Parable of the Sower" (Luke 8:4) and "The Parable of the Lamp" (Luke 8:16). He also explained how we should live in his "Sermon on the Plain" (Luke 6:20–26), which is the counterpart to St. Matthew's account of the "Sermon on the Mount" (Matthew 5:1–12). Jesus' life was about giving: he intervened wherever there was need: calming a storm at sea (Luke 8: 22–25); healing Jairus's daughter (Luke 8:40–48); and feeding the hungry five thousand (Luke 9:12–17); and he taught lessons that would lead his followers to eternal life: "The Parable of the Good Samaritan" (Luke 10:29–37); and the story, "Martha and Mary" (Luke 10:38–42).

While still in the midst of his teaching and healing, however, Jesus began to see the warning signs of impending doom in the questioning and criticism of the Pharisees and scholars of the law (Luke 11:37). Some of the Pharisees even came to Jesus and reported that the emperor Herod wanted to kill him; and yet, hoping in the kingdom of his Father, Jesus replied: *"Behold, I cast out demons and I perform healings today and tomorrow, and on the third day I accomplish my purpose. Yet I must continue on my way today, tomorrow, and the following day, for it is impossible that a prophet should die outside of Jerusalem"* (Luke 13:32–33).

As Jesus initiated the prophetic teaching ministry in Jerusalem his beliefs and actions began to be more and more questioned: *"Tell us, by what authority are you doing these things?"* (Luke 20:2). Ultimately Luke reports that a *conspiracy against Jesus* (Luke 22:1) has begun in earnest, including the betrayal of Judas (Luke 22:47–53); and the denial of

Peter (Luke 22:54–65). These led to the judgments of Pilate (Luke 23:1–5) and Herod (Luke 23:6–25), the way of the cross (Luke 23:26–32) and the crucifixion (Luke 23:33–49). Nevertheless, hope in his mission and in the Father's love was ever present even in Jesus' passion and death. These hopeful passages provide support and guidance for Christian nurses in their practice.

Luke describes three hope-filled expressions of Jesus, related to his experiences and interactions during the crucifixion. The first was immediately after Jesus had been nailed to the Cross between two criminals when he exclaimed: *"Father, forgive them, they know not what they do"* (Luke 23:34). The second was given in response to one of the men crucified with Jesus, who pleaded: *"Jesus, remember me when you come into your kingdom"* (Luke 23:42) and Jesus replied: *"Amen, I say to you, today you will be with me in Paradise"* (Luke 23:42–43). The third hope-filled comment of Jesus came as he recognized that the final throes of agony had at last arrived and he cried out with a loud voice: *"Father, into your hands I commend my spirit"* (Luke 23:46). As scripture scholar Carroll Stuhlmueller points out, Luke "removed the gloom and darkness from the death scene of Jesus; intense prayer and apostolic zeal dominate the last moments of the Savior's life."[5]

In Jesus' expression of compassion for those who *know not what they do,* "he utters the words of forgiveness that will become the hallmark of the innocent Christian sufferer."[6] In response to the "good thief" who seeks salvation, "Jesus promises him a place in paradise *today,* because the death of Jesus is beginning the exodus that will open a new way to salvation."[7] And Jesus' commitment of his life into the Father's hands is "a prayer of acceptance of the Father's will taken from Psalm 31:6" *("Into your hands I commend my spirit; you will redeem me, O LORD, O faithful God.")*.[8] Jesus' last words, asking his Father's forgiveness and promising salvation to a thief, as reported by Saint Luke, have rich analogies in the daily lives of Christian nurses.

Mary Ellen, a psychiatric-mental health nurse, told me a wonderful story about the "Father's forgiveness":

I was working in a psych (psychiatric) hospital, and I think, in a way I become a mediator between a patient and God. I was assigned to care for a young woman who had just had an abortion; she was suffering from severe postabortion depression and she was very angry at herself. She came from an Italian-Catholic family, went to a Catholic high school, was in the Legion of Mary and all that, and she thought that she had disgraced her family name. She thought that God would never forgive her.

For me, too, her behavior went against all I believe; I'm a very pro-life nurse. I didn't want to care for her. I thought my feelings about abortion would interfere with my nursing. So I prayed about it. I said: "God help me. You love this patient and you have forgiven her. Let me forgive her and let her forgive herself."

I met with the patient and mostly listened. She said: "Am I a bad person?" After my prayer I was able to tell her to think of God as a loving Father (her own father was very loving and he had forgiven her) and to ask his forgiveness. She could find peace in that; in God the Father's forgiveness. She said, "I feel so much better after talking to you."

And Ann, who worked in an inner-city hospital in a large metropolitan area, described one of her favorite patients, whom she labeled a *good thief*:

Horace was a "knight of the road"; was a "good thief." He was a head-and-neck surgery patient who had been a robber and had lived on the railroad tracks for years. I loved Horace. He died in our hospital and he was converted to Christianity before he died. He got past all the details of his life as a criminal to learn that God loved him. Horace was a witness to me because he was so simple and real and reflected God's love for us as sinners. He loved God and prayed all the time. Just like the good thief who was crucified with Jesus and repented at the end of his life, he knew that God had forgiven him. Horace wasn't complicated; God's forgiveness isn't complicated.

Luke notes that Jesus gave his life, as a final gesture of surrender "into his Father's hands." A hospice nurse, Sister Mary, told me that she believed nurses were especially blessed when they had the experience of passing dying patients "from their hands into God's hands." She told about twelve-year-old Teresa, who was dying from the invasion of a rapidly growing glioblastoma. Teresa was from a disadvantaged family who had great difficulty providing for her both emotionally and materially in the final stages of the illness. Sister Mary reported:

> So they brought her to us to die; they just couldn't cope any more. I cried a lot; I cried with the family. I cried for Teresa, who couldn't cry anymore. I felt so sorry for the parents; they couldn't watch her die. They said: "Sister, we're giving her into your hands." She died two days later.

Sister Mary added: "Before she died I kissed her and told her that we would love her and care for her. It was a special gift to get her ready to go into God's hands."

The evangelists Matthew and Mark identify only one sentence as being articulated by Jesus during his crucifixion. Matthew reports that the words were: "'Eli, Eli, lema sabachthani?' *which means 'My God, my God, why have you forsaken me?'*" (Matthew 27:46). Mark's version is only slightly different in the use of language: "'Eloi, Eloi, lema sabachthani' *which is translated 'My God, my God, why have you forsaken me?'*" (Mark 15:34). It is suggested that while Mark identified the words entirely in Aramaic, Matthew changed Jesus' "invocation of God to the Hebrew *Eli*," perhaps to correspond to a later verse about Elijah.[9]

What is most important, however, about Jesus' words: *"My God, my God, why have you forsaken me?"* is that they did not represent a cry of despair, but rather a continued affirmation of hope in his Father and his God. Jesus had not given up; he was, rather, in the tradition of his ancestors, calling on God whom he trusted to help him in this final hour of agony. Scripture scholars explain that Jesus' cry reflected the beginning of the Old Testament psalm of lament, Psalm 22: *"My God, my God, why have you forsaken me,/ far from my prayer, from the words of my cry* (v. 2)?" Psalm 22 is described as one of the most important of the Messianic psalms, "as Jesus prayed the psalm on the Cross," and as it describes so clearly his "spiritual and physical sufferings."[10] The psalm is not one of abandonment, however, but of hope, for while it describes "the Messiah's dereliction (vv. 2–6)," for example, v. 3: *"O my God, I cry out by day, and you answer not;/ by night, and there is no relief for me"*; "opprobrium (vv. 7–9)," for example, v. 8: *"All who see me scoff at me;/ they mock me with parted lips, they wag their heads"*; and "physical sufferings (vv. 13–19)," for example, v. 17: *"They have pierced my hands and my feet;/ I can count all my bones"*; it also identifies "his unshaken confidence in the heavenly Father" (v. 10: *"You have been my guide since I was first formed,/ my security at my mother's breast"*).[11]

Laments such as Psalm 22 were often verbalized by Hebrew persons who were suffering. The laments, "with their declaration of trust in God, were simultaneously prayers to God and testimonies of *hope* for the benefit of the community gathered around the one suffering."[12]

It is admitted that Jesus' praying of Psalm 22 during his Crucifixion (Matthew 27:46) does not negate an experience of suffering and loneliness: "In fact, the words of the psalm express most appropriately his feelings of abandonment and his subsequent reaffirmation of his total trust in the Father."[13] In commenting on the corresponding scripture passage in the gospel of Saint Mark (15:34), Van Linden asserts that Mark wanted his Christian readers "...to recognize in Jesus' last words and death the ultimate act of self-giving and trust....Mark's Jesus believes that God will hear him (Psalm 22:25) and will give him life, precisely because he suffered and died out of love and obedience."[14] Van Linden poses the rhetorical question: "Who would ever believe that life could come from death?" He continues: "Yet Mark wants his readers to believe that this is true, not only for Jesus but also for anyone who will follow in his steps."[15]

Hospice nurses know a lot about "life coming from death"; it's what keeps most of them going. Sister Mary validated that with another example:

There was this patient, Peggy—this young breast cancer patient with "mets" [metastasis] all over, and she had four little children. And she was dying. And one day I just sat beside her bed and I cried with her. I was so angry with God; I was furious at God. Peggy just wanted to live to see her little girl's first communion. I was so mad at why God would let this happen; I even said to him: "Take me and let her live to take care of her children." I was angry but I knew if anyone could handle my anger it was God. At first I felt she had been forsaken, but in the end I knew that God really loved Peggy very much. She had a wonderful husband and wonderful children. She gave them so much in her last months and they are living that today. She gave life even in her death.

The evangelist John, whose gospel is believed to have been written last, added three new comments to those previously identified as having been spoken by Jesus during the crucifixion:

When Jesus saw his mother and the disciple there whom he loved, he said to his mother, *"Woman, behold your son."* Then he said to the disciple, *"Behold your mother."*
John 19:26–27 (emphasis added)

Aware that everything was now finished, in order that the scriptures might be fulfilled, Jesus said, *"I thirst."*
John 19:28 (emphasis added)

When Jesus had taken the wine, he said, *"It is finished."* And bowing his head, he handed over the spirit.
John 19:30 (emphasis added)

While a literal interpretation of John 20:26–27 seems to be related to Jesus' concern for his mother, commentators note that Mary might have been identified as a figure of the church or as the mother of all Christians; this moment may symbolize the birth of Christianity.[16]

I love the concept of Mary as mother of all of us, because a mother's love is so tender and so embracing and so faithful. I saw the love of Jesus' mother beautifully reflected in many mothers of young men living with AIDS. One of my special memories is of Agnes. Although she herself was suffering from a number of physical problems, she had supported her son Michael through all the stages of his illness. When Michael was dying in the hospital, the furthest Agnes would go from his side was the unit waiting room; and she went only when forced to leave so that the nurses could carry out their care. One evening I asked Agnes how she could manage the long hours of watching and waiting at Michael's bedside. She looked at me rather curiously that I should pose such a question, and she replied simply but with great conviction, "Michael is my only son; he's my heart. Where else could I be?"

Jesus' admission *"I thirst."* has been associated, as has his cry, *"Eloi, Eloi, lema sabachthani,"* with the Messianic Psalm 22; in this case with verses 15–16: *"I am like water poured out;.../My throat is dried up like clay, my tongue cleaves to my jaws;/ to the dust of death you have brought me down."*

I wonder if Jesus was thirsting only for water, which surely he needed, or also for compassion and care at the height of his suffering. Caring is what so many of those we nurse thirst for, especially persons who are marginalized from our larger society. An emergency room nurse, Sarah, described her struggle to "quench" this kind of thirst:

> One of the biggest problems we had in our E.R. was with the "street people" who come in with all kinds of made-up complaints. They came in droves when it was cold or rainy; they would start arriving as soon as it got dark. One I remember especially was Charlie. He would arrive around midnight, spend the night, and then hit the road in the morning. He was charming but dirty and reeked of wine; he had all kinds of unreal complaints. He would demand: "I want to see the nurse." Mostly I wanted to say, "Charlie can't you see I'm busy; get out of here!" But we began to realize that what Charlie (and all the other "Charlies") really wanted, what they really were hungry and thirsty for, was some attention, some human companionship and care, some comfort. So we set up a room near the E.R. just for them, with coffee

and sandwiches, where they could come and sit at night and be together.

And, finally, Jesus' words *"It is finished"* can be interpreted to mean that his work on earth had been accomplished: "the will of his Father, the Scriptures, the salvation of humankind."[17] The evangelist John seems to indicate that Jesus was at peace with the ending of his earthly life in his assertion that Jesus simply lowered his head and gave his spirit to the Father. For Jesus, God's divine Son, there would be no raging against the dying light.

The elders, with whom I worked in several nursing home studies, also taught me about finding peace in the fact of one's life being "finished." One woman I remember was eighty-seven-year-old Mrs. Catherine McAuliff. Although she had a loving extended family, she had chosen to be admitted to the nursing home when her health and physical strength began to fail. Catherine told me: "I don't want to ever be a burden on my children. This is a peaceful place for me to be. My life was a good life. I tried to do God's will and now it's finished. I can go to him whenever he's ready. I'm in his hands now; I'm just waiting for his time."

In sum, all of Jesus' words during his passion, as recorded by the four evangelists, contain within them a message of hope and trust that sets the example for his followers. While pain and sorrow in this world are something a Christian will have to face, as reflected in the nursing anecdotes related above, hope for eternal life with the Father will provide the strength to deal with such suffering. For Christian nurses this hope is not only a personal joy and comfort, but also a necessary tool for helping patients cope with the stresses of illness and disability.

"I Raise My Eyes toward the Mountains"

Over and over the beautiful psalms, the prayers that Jesus prayed, remind us to hope in the promise of God's protection and sustenance for his people. One of my favorites is Psalm 121: "The Lord Our Guardian":

I lift up my eyes toward the mountains;
whence shall help come to me?
My help is from the LORD,
who made heaven and earth.
May he not suffer your foot to slip;
may he slumber not who guards you:
Indeed he neither slumbers nor sleeps,
the guardian of Israel.
The LORD is your guardian; the LORD is your shade;
he is beside you at your right hand.
The sun shall not harm you by day,
nor the moon by night.
The LORD will guard you from all evil;
he will guard your life.
The LORD will guard your coming and your going,
both now and forever.

When I was very small I had one of those wonderful snow globes that children love. When the globe is still, the snow lies hidden at the base of the glass sphere, but when shaken, a snow storm magically appears to transform the image displayed within. The tiny figurine in my snow globe depicted a scene reflective of the message of Psalm 121. The globe contained three connected figures: a little boy and a little girl holding hands while crossing a footbridge over a dangerous looking ravine. Behind the children and embracing them with widespread protective wings was a lovely angel of God with golden hair. I spent many playtimes making the snow storm rage so that I could enjoy watching the children, under the guardianship of their angel, emerge safely out of the flurries.

This morning when I was meditating on Psalm 121, I remembered my childhood snow globe and the joy I had in looking at the small children protected by their guardian angel. Sometimes I think it's too bad we have to grow up; at least in terms of the faith dimension of our lives. The psalmist, who authored Psalm 121, was perhaps trying to tell us that. What a wonderful thing it is to know that our loving Father will not allow our *"foot to slip"* from whatever path we happen to be on; to know that God is our *guardian* who *"never slumbers nor sleeps."* We're never alone on this foot-bridge of life, so often traversing dangerous gullies and cre-vasses. We are embraced by the protecting arms of our *Guardian* who will allow neither the light nor the darkness to harm us. He who guards our *"coming and going"* will protect us as we begin a task and as we come to its end. He will always watch over our lives.

In the preceding chapter I mentioned some of the rocky ravines or desert places, such as suffering, fear and pain, over which or through which we, as nurses, must pass. There are others. For each of us the difficulties will be personalized. But that is no problem for our Guardian, who knows the depth of each heart, which he alone can fully understand. What a won-derful source of strength is Psalm 121 if we trust the inspired word of God that he will protect us from all evil. It's true, of course, that some things happen in our lives as nurses that surely may seem to be less than good: having to watch a young mother die of cancer; experiencing a feeling of failure in not being able to alleviate the hopelessness of a drug-addicted teen; or being forced to encounter the pain and frustration of parents whose child is suffering from a life-threatening illness. It is precisely in situations like these, however, that we need to remember the protecting arms of the Lord, our Guardian; that we need to cry out to him, in our pain and our anger and our fear. That we need, in our helplessness, to *"raise our eyes to the mountains,"* from whence comes our help, and lean our heads on the strong shoulder of the One who will guard our *"coming and going, both now and forever."*

"I Will Listen to You"

> For I know well the plans I have in mind for you, says the LORD; plans for your welfare, not for woe! plans to give you a future full of hope. When you call me, when you go to pray to me, I will listen to you. When you look for me, you will find me. Yes, when you seek me with all your heart, you will find me with you, says the LORD.
>
> Jeremiah 29:11–14

There is a multiplicity of references to the importance of prayer in both the Old and New Testament scriptures. The prophet Jeremiah makes the case for the Lord very directly and very simply with the message: *"...when you pray to me I will listen to you"* and *"when you seek me with all your heart you will find me with you."* For more than that we surely could not ask. God is promising us both his listening and his presence if we pray to him with all our hearts. There is a plethora of spiritual and religious books and articles describing prayer: the value of and need for prayer; techniques of prayer; hindrances to prayer and so forth. There are books of prayers for various occasions; there are even books of prayer for those who care for the sick. My purpose here, however, is not to attempt any in-depth exploration of the various kinds of prayer for nurses. I would simply like to consider prayer as a dimension of the nurse' strength for I believe that, in fact, it is one of a nurse's greatest sources of energy and renewal in times of stress and suffering; it is one of a nurse's greatest sources of joy and comfort during times of peace and prosperity.

The word *prayer* is frequently equated with the concept of petition. This petition is usually thought of as being made to God or one of his representatives.[18] Other kinds of prayer include activities such as adoration, meditation or contemplation. There are many different styles of prayer that can be helpful to nurses during a busy workday. For some of us beginning the day with a time of formalized prayer or worship sets a tone of being in the presence of the Lord. While there most probably will not be any significant block of time for formal prayer during a nurse's workday, briefly bringing to one's consciousness the presence of God can be very comforting. Trappistine Sister Miriam Pollard suggests that "little chinks in the day" can be used for prayer: "...not trying to cram as many prayers into a day as you can, but reaching out gently to touch the hand of God, or simply to be aware of His presence."[19] To "hold God's hand...is not a childish luxury," according to Dr. Gerald May.[20] To hold God's hand for even a brief moment may give a nurse the strength to carry on in the face of significant sorrow or suffering.

Some days I can only find a longer period of time to pray in the evening, at the end of a very busy day. And at that time my head and my heart are often very full—full of problems, full of experiences, full of plans, or full of worries. It's hard to settle down and just be with God. And yet I know that this is precisely the time when I need to listen to the Lord. For surely my dearest Friend, my deepest love, my constant companion, the center of my life is the one to whom I can bring my concerns, no matter how small or insignificant they may seem.

Recently, at an evening prayer service, the priest-presider told us about his high school infatuation with fifteen-year-old Samantha. He admitted: "I thought about her all the time. I couldn't wait to be with her. I wanted to talk to her. I wanted her to talk to me. I couldn't get her out of my mind; I was infatuated!" Then he looked around at the assembled congregation and said, with a smile: "God is infatuated with you! He can't get you out of his mind. He can't wait for you to come to him; to spend time with him. He's head-over-heels in love with you." What a wonderful invitation and introduction to prayer. I sometimes get afraid that God will get tired of my prayers; I seem to keep describing the same needs and concerns over and over. That's the error we humans so often make in our relationship with God. We try to make him in our image and likeness instead of the other way around! And all he wants is that we come to him as a Father, with trusting and loving hearts; he will do the rest.

Some evenings, when I'm really tired, I try not to talk at God, but just to be with him and to listen. Those are usually my best times of prayer; the nonprogrammed, spontaneous kind. When I'm not worrying, or asking or even thanking, but just letting God do the leading. Those are the times when my mind and heart are quiet enough to hear the soft, gentle whisperings of his Spirit; to be still and experience the peace and joy of knowing that he is God. This is the greatest gift God gives to us in prayer.

The Nurse's Cloister

"Every Ward into a Church"

A friend who works as a nurse-anesthetist in a large city hospital wrote to me last year and said: "I've been so busy lately; things never seem to slow down." She explained that between managing her job, her family and her volunteer responsibilities, her life had been moving at a frantic pace. She closed her note with the exclamation: "I need a *cloister!*" Knowing my friend as well as I do, knowing how she practices her nursing and especially how she lives the gospel message of Jesus, I'm certain that there is much *cloister* mentality incorporated into her days, although she may not perceive this is the midst of the busyness.

The word *cloister* is defined by Livingstone as "an enclosed space which normally forms the central part of a monastery or other religious building."[21] It may also be understood as "any place where one can lead a secluded life."[22] My nurse-anesthetist friend was probably thinking of a secluded, religious space when she expressed her need for a cloister. And in truth we all do need those cloistered times, whether it involves going away to a monastic setting for a retreat or a day of recollection, or even simply spending a few quiet hours in a local church or place of prayer. But what I would like to suggest here is that perhaps, in between those special times, a nurse may, during her ordinary working day, find the occasional few minutes of cloister in a health care setting. In chapter three I reported the suggestions of several staff nurses who gave examples of times and settings in which they might be able to snatch a few minutes for quiet prayer and reflection. The attempt to incorporate one's spirituality with one's professional activities was supported from nursing's inception by our foundress, Florence Nightingale, who, in speaking to a group of nursing students, asserted: *"And I pray God that he will make through you, every ward into a church; and teach us how to be the Gospel [which is] the only way to preach the Gospel."*[23]

There is a similar concept, articulated in a famous quotation attributed to Saint Vincent de Paul, in which he told his newly founded religious community, the Daughters of Charity: "Your convent will be the house of the sick; your cloister the wards of the hospital."[24] Vincent and the cofounder of the Daughters, Louise De Marillac, realized well that, considering the tenuous health care milieu of seventeenth-century Paris, their newly formed band of sister-nurses would have precious little time or energy to spend praying in a formal cloister. Vincent was a saint, but he was also a pragmatist. He advised the sisters that if they were called to care for a sick person while at prayer, they should answer the call with joy; his instruction was that when this occurred the sisters would be leaving God to go to God.

There are many times when we as nurses would love to have a cloistered place of prayer to escape to. When this is not possible, however, we might try, as Vincent de Paul and Florence Nightingale taught, to find our cloister in the sickroom, the clinic or the wards of the hospital. We might try to learn, if we have to leave God in formal prayer, to go to God in the person of our patients.

A Christmas Candle

The Companionship of God

Candles are meaningful and treasured symbols for people of diverse cultures and diverse faith beliefs. Candles are lit to celebrate significant life occurrences, such as birthdays, graduations, weddings, anniversaries and funerals. Candles are used to decorate the home for festive holiday occasions or to acknowledge the presence of special guests at one's table. And for some individuals, candles are burned simply to signify an atmosphere of peace and reflection. One of the most important uses of candles, of course, has to do with their religious symbolism.

I love candles, but I don't often light one when I'm alone. I'm not sure why; perhaps it's my parsimonious Irish nature. But last Christmas season I violated that norm. It was Christmas Eve, a day usually filled with family or community activities like last-minute shopping, food preparation or visiting friends who are sick or homebound. This year, however, I had gotten myself into a real time bind in terms of a writing task. When, the preceding summer, I had signed a book contract promising my publisher a completed manuscript by December 31st, I imagined that the work would be finished long before that date. Why I agreed to a deadline so close to Christmas Day I do not know. At any rate, I found myself, on the morning of December 24th, looking at a final chapter that was only half completed. Panic began to set in. In addition to the panic, an overwhelming loneliness set in, for I realized, without a doubt, that in order to get the manuscript in on time I would have to put most of my energy into writing during the coming week. My desire for compliance with my publisher's deadline was at war with my desire to experience the spirituality and the joy of the season—to feel the blessedness of the advent of the birth of Jesus. It seemed that I couldn't have it both ways. Or could I?

Suddenly I remembered a beautiful Christmas candle that a dear friend had brought me from a trip to the Holy Land the previous summer. It was a lovely tall white candle with a small Nativity scene engraved in bright colors on the front. After duly admiring the candle, I had wrapped it carefully in tissue and tucked it away to be used to celebrate some distant and as yet unnamed future occasion. The occasion, I decided, was now!

I retrieved my Christmas candle and placed it in a small glass holder on the worktable next to my computer. As I lit the candle I asked God to bless this Christmas Eve of writing. Even though I'm not a very good typist, my fingers seemed to fly through those beginning paragraphs. But that was not the best part. My special Christmas present was the fact that the first time I looked up from my work and admired the beauty and warmth of the slender orange flame, I was reminded of St. John of the Cross's image of Jesus as the *living flame of love*. With a rush of joy I realized that I was not at all alone in my work on that Christmas Eve; I was accompanied by the *strength* and the support and the tender care of the God who is ever at my side. I understood that my friend's gift of the Christmas candle was only a symbol of the real gift, the Light of the world, who came to us in a stable at Bethlehem almost two thousand years ago. Caryll Houselander has observed that what Jesus really wishes is "to be thought of as a candle burning in a little room; to be the secret light tended in His true home, the human heart."[25] My writing took on a new and special meaning that Christmas Eve; I was filled with peace and gratitude for the treasure of Jesus' love and the warmth of his companionship each time I glanced at the symbolic flame. I kept my Christmas candle burning until the chapter was completed, the glow of its flame reminiscent of the beckoning star of Bethlehem.

This chapter has been about nurses' strength; about nurses' hope in the Lord, which will enable them to *"run and not grow weary,"* to *"walk and not faint."* God is the nurse's hope; God is the nurse's strength; God is the nurse's constant companion. In prayer the nurse will receive the strength to love and to care and to hope with those who are ill. In prayer nurses will find their ability to *"soar as with eagles' wings."*

CHAPTER 6.
WHERE YOUR
TREASURE IS:

The Nurse's Reward

"Store up treasures in heaven...for where your treasure is there also will your heart be."
—*Matthew 6:20–21*

In his first-century gospel Matthew presented us with what today is an accepted principle—that one's heart will be focused on and one's energies directed toward that which is considered most important in life, that which is *treasured*. While the majority of us complain of not having enough time to manage our perceived responsibilities, most will admit to making time for those things that we treasure. For some the treasures are myriad, centered in such arenas as church, family, job, community or education. Whatever professional accomplishments, social groups, or formal organizations we consider important, however, our most valuable and most profound treasure, the treasure of which Matthew wrote in his gospel, is the spiritual treasure of God's love.

Matthew's advice is so practical for the contemporary Christian: *"Do not store up for yourselves treasures on earth, where moth and decay destroy and thieves break in and steal. But store up treasures in heaven, where neither moth nor decay destroy, nor thieves break in and steal"* (vv. 19–20).

Those of us who are city dwellers, especially, spend a lot of time strategizing as how best to protect our earthly "treasures" from urban "thieves" and "moths." We install sophisticated burglar alarm systems in our homes; we park our cars with steel antitheft devices locked across the steering wheels; we purchase a multiplicity of guarantees, warranties and insurance policies to secure the safety and functioning of our belongings.

Recently, in an attempt to simplify my lifestyle, I significantly decreased my living space. Concurrently, of course, I had to significantly decrease the number of my possessions; all of that precious "stuff" that I had guarded so carefully from the clutches of Matthew's *"moths"* and *"thieves."* The result has been an incredible sense of freedom and peace. I now have many fewer material things to worry about and much more time to enjoy the real *treasures* with which God has blessed me: my church, my family and friends, my work, the beauty of nature and, most importantly, God's love and presence in my life.

I'm firmly convinced that Matthew has got it right; we need to look into our hearts, deep into our hearts, and we will find there the gift that is the treasure of God's love—the magnificent treasure that we don't ever have to worry about losing. We will recognize, without a doubt, where our treasure truly is. For us as nurses, Matthew's message has special importance. In the practice of nursing we face continually and consistently the "theft" and "decay" of physiological or psychological functioning, or sometimes both, in our fragile patients. If our hearts are focused on the treasures of this world, on earthly or material pleasures and goods, facing the losses associated with illness and disability will be overwhelming. If we acknowledge the love of God as our greatest possession, such losses take on a very different level of importance.

Storing Treasures

Nurse-Patient Interaction

In my years of interviewing nurses some of the best stories describing the *rewards* of our profession have reflected instances of nurse-patient interaction. Of course there are rewards associated with nursing activities such as teaching, writing, or conducting research; all of these contribute to the field. But the spirituality of human contact, of one heart reaching out to another heart and experiencing in the interaction the presence of God, provides for most of us the greatest satisfaction and the greatest joy. When I was interviewing nurses who had cared for persons living with the human immunodeficiency virus (HIV), I heard moving reports of loving service provided. Generally, however, the point that the nurse caregivers emphasized in telling their stories related not to the service they had given but rather to the perception of how much they had received in working with those living with the virus. In fact, I could identify many tremendously rewarding instances in my own clinical nursing research with HIV-positive persons. Perhaps one of the most treasured experiences was an interaction that I had with Christopher several months after his friend Jonathan's death from *pneumocystis carinii* pneumonia.

Christopher had invited me to dinner at a small quiet restaurant near his home; the agenda was to discuss the bereavement experience, as well as his own HIV positivity. After our meal Christopher offered to walk me to the train station, a short distance away. It was a lovely brisk evening in mid-December, and there were fine snowflakes blowing across our faces as we traversed the few blocks to the station. As we walked along the downtown street, my arm linked in Christopher's, he gently headed us toward a local record shop. We entered the store, continuing our reminiscences about Jonathan, while Christopher chose a cassette recording. When we returned to the street he handed me the small package; it contained a tape of Bette Midler's *Beaches,* which included the music for the song: "The Wind Beneath My

Wings." This was the song that Christopher had selected to be played at Jonathan's memorial service. Christopher looked at me, his eyes brimming with tears, and said: "Thank you for being 'The Wind Beneath My Wings' during these months since Jonathan's death." I replied: "Thank you for being 'The Wind Beneath My Wings' also." We stood in the middle of the busy avenue, hugging and crying, as Christmas shoppers detoured around us. That cassette recording was one of the best Christmas presents I have ever received. It reminded me that in my work with those who are most fragile it has truly been the patients and their families, as God's instruments, who have helped me to understand and to treasure the sacredness of human life, who have provided me with the inspiration and the courage to continue in the face of painful losses.

It is in human interaction that we make living the treasure of Jesus in our hearts and in our lives. In his classic work *Reaching Out*, Henri Nouwen tells the story of a spiritual interaction with a former student. After spending some quiet time together the student observed that when he looked at Henri he felt as if he was in the presence of Christ. Nouwen replied: "It is the Christ in you, who recognizes the Christ in me."[1]

A Sacramental Moment

One day a Sister of Mercy friend of mine, Sister Teresa, was describing her work with homeless women at an urban inner-city health care facility. "What we do is sacrament!" she exclaimed. "Explain what you mean by *sacrament?*" I asked her. "Well," she replied "You see Jesus in the person you care for. Jesus is in you and in that person. There is a grace there. You may see the wounded Jesus, the rejoicing Jesus, the suffering Jesus, depending on the circumstances." Being ever the researcher, I prodded her to give me an example, to tell me more about what she meant by the term *sacrament*. "OK," she said. "The other day there was this woman lying on the floor in the homeless shelter; she was in terrible shape. We cleaned her; we took her to the hospital. Then we came back and we cleaned up her room; it was really bad. This may not be nursing per se but it is caring for the patient's environment and making a home for her to come back to." Sister Teresa continued: "Two of us went to the hospital with her to make sure they paid attention to her; it's like you think of the fifth station of the cross, when Simon of Cyrene went along with Jesus. Her cross was just too heavy to carry alone; we were really walking along with Jesus. That was a *sacramental moment* for us as nurses."

After my discussion with Sister Teresa, I began to ponder the concept of sacramental moments; how many of them we as nurses really do have in the course of our daily practice. How many we never recognize in the midst of our busyness. A secular definition of *sacrament* suggests that it is "something that has the significance of a deeply religious act or observance."² According to Saint Thomas Aquinas a sacrament is "the sign of a sacred thing in so far as it sanctifies men."³ And speaking liturgically, Kevin Irwin describes a Christian sacrament as providing the participants with an "experience [of] the paschal mystery of Christ."⁴ All three of these explanations of sacrament have relevance for nursing.

The concept of "religious act or observance" generally brings to mind an activity carried out in a church or a pastoral care setting; sometimes the action is guided by an individual trained in theological or spiritual matters. Nevertheless, a nursing behavior such as the sharing of personal prayer is also a deeply *"religious act,"* yet may be undertaken in a health care setting together with a patient or family member. Nurses report that praying with a patient is one of the most *sacred* experiences they encounter in their practice. Shared prayer not only offers a dimension of spiritual care to patients, but provides, in the words of Aquinas, *"a sign of the sacred"* that *sanctifies* the nurse as well.

For the Christian nurse, praying with patients can also lead to an *"experience of the paschal mystery"* in allowing both the patient and nurse to consciously bring Jesus into their midst. For as he promised, *"Where two or three are gathered together in my name, there am I in the midst of them"* (Matthew 18:20).

Physician and spiritual writer Gerald May speaks of the "sacrament of the present moment," which he explains is derived from the writings of the French Jesuit Jean-Pierre de Caussade, who observed: "There are no moments which are not filled with God's infinite holiness so that there are none we should not honor."[5] In discussing the spirituality of nurses' work, William Droel questions whether nursing is a vocation with a sacramental dimension or simply a job.[6] In response Droel quotes the director of nursing of an urban hospital, who asserts that there is a "very special and sacramental" nature to nursing activities, which may take place during "a significant time in people's lives."[7]

Holding a Sacredness

In describing the spiritual rewards of caregiving, Andrew who had worked extensively with the terminally ill, described his patient interactions as "holy places we share when we have time together." Andrew explained: "There is a sweetness in being with these persons even when they are very ill and death is immanent; it gives one the incredible sense of *holding a sacredness*."[8]

The word *sacred* has been variously defined as meaning: "set apart for the service or worship of the deity; worthy of religious veneration; holy; and relating to religion."[9] In *The New Dictionary of Catholic Spirituality* no specific definition is given for the term *sacred;* the reader is advised instead to explore the concepts: *God, holiness* and *mystery*.[10] For most of us the term *sacred* or *sacredness* evokes religious or spiritual images. One thinks of places or things that reflect transcendence, that are related to God or to eternity. The imaging of sacredness in our personal lives is also often reserved for specifically religious times or experiences. We think of sacredness as associated with such activities as attendance at worship services, undertaking of private prayer or meditation, or periods of religious retreat. On more occasions than I care to recount, I have found myself rushing through some ostensibly secular activities in order to get to the *sacred*. But what in fact is it that distinguishes the secular from the sacred for a follower of Jesus? For should not God be central to all of the experiences and actions of our lives? Or in the words of De Caussade is not each moment "filled with God's infinite holiness?"

One morning several months ago, while driving to Mass, I pondered the *sacredness* of my ordinary morning activities. My musings led to a memory of many years ago, when I wore a religious habit. My community had a tradition of reciting a prayer as we donned each part of the garb: the tunic, the cincture, the cape, the rosary and the veil. The rationale for our dressing prayer was that one was clothing oneself in preparation for a day in the service of the Lord. Why then, I reasoned, although I no longer wear a habit, would it not still be appropriate to ask the Lord's blessing each morning as I dress? As in the past, the prayer could serve to reflect both for myself and before God that indeed this is a "day which the Lord has made." I have initiated the practice and find joy and comfort in this small ritual of preparing for each new day in God's service. A simple act, yet holding within it the seeds of sacredness.

St. Augustine, in his classic prayer "Late Have I Loved Thee," acknowledges the sacredness of God's involvement in every aspect of creation in the words: *"Created things kept me from You; yet if they had not been in You, they would not have been at all."* For those who care for the sick, God's presence may seem very close in some created things, especially in issues related to such significant life changes as birth and death. When dealing with the ordinary or the frustrating, however, the patient who never seems satisfied with his care, the coworker who never seems to pull her weight, the hospital administrator who always seems to choose the midst of a crisis for a visit, finding the sacredness may be more difficult. It is in these situations that the Christian nurse can derive strength and courage from the gospel message of a crucified Jesus, from the word and commitment of the Son of God, who understood so well human frailty and human suffering and who promised his disciples: *"Come to me, all you who labor and are burdened, and I will give you rest. Take my yoke upon you and learn from me, for I am meek and humble of heart; and you will find rest for yourselves. For my yoke is easy, and my burden light"* (Matthew 11:28–30).

Mary and Martha

As they continued their journey [Jesus] entered a village where a woman whose name was Martha welcomed him. She had a sister named Mary [who] sat beside the Lord at his feet listening to him speak. Martha, burdened with much serving, came to him and said: "Lord, do you not care that my sister has left me by myself to do the serving? Tell her to help me." The Lord said to her in reply, "Martha, Martha, you are anxious and worried about many things. There is need of only one thing. Mary has chosen the better part and it will not be taken from her."

Luke 10:38–42

The parable of Martha and Mary teaches "a discipleship that abandons the cares of this world, even the obligations of hospitality, for the one thing necessary to salvation—hearing and keeping the word of Jesus."[11] The narrative illustrates the fact that "the whole gospel is not contained in loving service to others, no matter how important that is."[12] Following Jesus' commandment to seek first the kingdom of God is the central responsibility of a Christian.

In my younger years I struggled mightily with Luke's depiction of the Mary and Martha parable. What troubled me most were the words, *"Mary has chosen the better part."* "What about poor Martha?" I would complain, "slaving away in the kitchen (I presume they had kitchens in those days) so that Jesus and Mary could have something to eat?" It surely didn't seem fair that Mary got applauded for just sitting around.

As I have lived longer, however, I have come to realize why Luke was so insistent on emphasizing the concept of spiritual nourishment, which can only be obtained by sitting at the feet of Jesus. The words of Jesus are the food that is necessary to sustain the Christian.

We, as nurses, tend to be activity oriented. During a work day, whether in a patient's home, a clinic, a hospital or a university, there are many tasks that need to be accomplished in our commitment to care for the sick. Nevertheless, contemporary nurses do fairly well in regard to nourishing their minds and their bodies. We have learned the importance of continuing education to support our practice. We accept the positive benefits of exercise and good nutrition in providing us with physical energy. But the spirit, the life-giving principle of mind and body, is sometimes neglected. Like Martha, we can always identify a task that needs to be done, and we feel good and productive in its accomplishment. But there are days when it seems almost impossible to find the time to *sit at Jesus' feet* as Mary did—that is, until we truly identify where our treasure lies.

Last year, at the end of a three-day retreat, I spoke with a critical-care nurse, Patrice, about her experience. The retreat was made in silence, a period that I like to call "Mary time"—sitting at the feet of Jesus. Patrice's first comment was, "I can't believe how much I needed that!" She explained how difficult it was to find quiet time in light of her busy schedule. Patrice also admitted that after the days of retreat, she recognized the value of contemplative prayer. She planned to continue the practice.

In an article on biblical servanthood, Kathy Schoonover-Shoffner discussed the nurse's call to be a *Mary* or a *Martha*. She observed that nurses can "get stuck rallying around service rather than focusing on the one we serve."[13] The key to such service for a Christian nurse lies, I believe, in making a conscious intention to carry out our practice in the name of and for the sake of Jesus the Lord. Nurses, as all busy professionals, will probably always have a Martha-Mary struggle when scheduling their activities. The continued awareness of this, however, may not be a bad thing. In fact Trappist Basil Pennington teaches that "the Martha-Mary tension should live in all of us because it lives in the teaching of Christ."[14] Father Basil explains that such tension is positive because it "challenges us constantly to examine our lives and our fidelity

to the word."[15] It's all right there in the greatest commandment, as Mark reminds us:

> *One of the scribes...asked [Jesus], "Which is the first of all
> the commandments?" Jesus replied, "The first is this: 'Hear,
> O Israel! The Lord our God is Lord alone! You shall love the
> Lord your God with all your heart, with all your soul, with
> all your mind, and with all your strength.' The second is
> this: 'You shall love your neighbor as yourself.' There is no
> other commandment greater than these."* (12:28–31)

The Nurse's Reward

> *"Fear Not Abram! I am your shield;
> I will make your reward very great."*
> Genesis 15:1

The story of the patriarch Abraham, as recorded in the Old
Testament Book of Genesis, reveals a man beloved of God yet
beset with trials and sufferings. First of all, Abram's wife,
Sarai, for many years appeared barren (Genesis 11:30); this
was a great disappointment in an era when honor and wealth
were determined through one's descendants. Then, at the
age of seventy-five, Abram was asked by God to leave his
home and his kinsmen and migrate to a land he had never
seen (Genesis 12:1). Without a word of complaint, Abram
packed his bags and set out together with Sarai (Genesis
12:4–6). After a significant number of geographical reloca-
tions, turf battles and interpersonal family problems, God
promised Abram that his *reward would be very great* (Genesis
15:1). God assured him that he would have many possessions
and even heirs. But still Sarai was barren.

Finally, when he was ninety-nine years old, God made a
covenant with Abram, changing his name to Abraham and
promising that he would become the father of a "host of
nations" (Genesis 17:1–8). God also announced that Sarai's
name should be changed to Sarah and that she would give
birth, at ninety, to a son to be named Isaac (Genesis

17:15–19). God promised to maintain his covenant with Isaac and all of his descendants.

Abraham had traveled many miles, enduring numerous difficulties in the service of the Lord, and he "was one hundred years old when Isaac was born" (Genesis 21:5). One would think that after all of his struggles, Abraham, now an old man, could sit back and enjoy raising Isaac, yet one more trial awaited him. God said to Abraham: *"Take your son Isaac, your only one, whom you love, and go to the land of Moriah. There you shall offer him up as a holocaust"* (Genesis 22:2). As we know from the story, Abraham had prepared the altar for sacrifice and bound his son when, at the last minute, God intervened saying: *"Because you acted as you did in not withholding from me your beloved son, I will bless you abundantly"* (Genesis 22:16–17). Abraham was promised many rewards during the remainder of his life.

In examining the Old Testament account of Abraham's spiritual journey we find three foci in the narrative: God's commitment, Abraham's trust, and a multiplicity of obstacles that tested the patriarch's trusting in the Lord. At the time of the greatest trial, however, that of being asked to sacrifice Isaac, Abraham was shown to be "fully obedient to God's will."[16] It has been suggested that Abraham's faith in God was such that "he believed him able to raise (Isaac) to life again."[17] Abraham's call and response are significant for Christians in the historical context of God meeting "human beings at one time and one place,"[18] and because, in fact, "we are all children of Abraham."[19] Ultimately, the narrative teaches that "God blessed Abraham and made him his specially chosen friend because Abraham was faithful to God."[20]

So what does the Genesis account of Abraham have to say to us as contemporary practitioners of nursing? A great deal, I think, not only in terms of *reward* but also in alerting us to the trials and obstacles that may precede our openness to receiving God's gifts; to becoming God's *specially chosen friends.* From God's first call Abraham obeyed without question, yet he was faced with difficulty after difficulty throughout his life. And isn't that the way our lives sometimes seem to be going? On the good days, we may experience peace and gratitude for our call to be nurses: on the days when we have the joy of watching two young parents pick up their initially fragile neonate, now well enough to be discharged from the neonatal intensive care unit; or when one of our former chemotherapy patients drops by to let us know how well she's doing and to show us how pretty her newly regrown head of hair looks. These are days of *reward*. But then there are also many of the difficult days: the days when none of our patients seem to appreciate our efforts in their behalf; or the days when our own health or family problems threaten to prevent us from continuing to respond to our call to care. When a trial becomes particularly challenging, the story of Abraham, who had faith enough to be willing to sacrifice his only son, can encourage us to trust and to be obedient to the will of God, no matter how painful or impossible such a response may seem. We will be able to trust because we have learned where our treasure truly is.

CHAPTER 7.
THAT THEY MAY
HAVE LIFE:

Nursing's Call to Reverence

---

*"I come so that they might have life and have it
more abundantly."*
—John 10:10

While attending a pro-life conference at the Basilica of the
National Shrine of the Immaculate Conception, I heard
Mother Agnes Mary Donovan, S.V., Superior General of the
Sisters of Life, speak about the concept of reverence, most
notably reverence for the sacredness of human life. One of
the questions Mother Agnes Mary posed, as a criterion measure of reverence, especially captured my nurse's heart: *"Do I,
in my behavior, honor and bring dignity to those who are compromised by illness or by age and leave them with an experience
of their worth before God?"*

Days after the meeting I continued to ruminate about
Mother Agnes Mary's question, which seemed to have

caught hold of me with a vengeance that would not let go. Around the same time I also attended our university's baccalaureate commitment to nursing, or "capping" ceremony. Although capping is considered by some to be an anachronism, our students continue to request the ceremony as they enter into their clinical experiences. In the ritual the nurses' caps are blessed by the university chaplain prior to being placed on the students' heads. Each nursing student then receives a lighted candle, and a prayer, composed jointly by the class, is recited. Reverence dominates the ceremony.

Perhaps because my captivation with the concept of reverence would not go away; perhaps also because the students' reverent capping ceremony took place in the same basilica where Mother Agnes Mary's question had moved my heart, I decided that I needed to explore what the term *reverence* really means for us as nurses. I undertook a concept analysis by examining both the nursing and theological/spiritual literature on reverence, and by documenting experiences of reverence in caregiving as reported by practicing nurses.

The Spiritual Meaning of *Reverence*

The synonyms for *reverence* found in an unabridged Webster's dictionary seem to suggest both a secular and a sacred understanding of the word; the concepts identified include: respect, obeisance, esteem, admiration, homage, worship and adoration.[1] The word *reverence* is derived from the Latin *reverentia* and is described as incorporating "profound respect mingled with love and awe as for a holy or exalted being."[2] Definitions of *reverence* discussed in the theological dictionaries tend to focus on the honor and worship of God and, by extension, those persons and things that God has created.

The *Encyclopedic Dictionary of Religion* explains the theological meaning of reverence as related to both justice and charity toward those who provide and care for one. Reverence, has, however, "its highest form of expression of indebtedness toward God as the source of all being and goodness."[3] This understanding is supported by *The New Catholic Encyclopedia,* which describes *reverence* as a "virtue inclining man to satisfy his obligation of respect" to those in authority;[4] and *The New Dictionary of Sacramental Worship,* in which *reverence* is presented as "a relational stance of deep respect before a person, or by extension any reality, that is held to be sacred or worthy of honor."[5]

In his encyclical letter, *Evangelium Vitae, The Gospel of Life,* the Holy Father speaks of the importance of reverence for life on the part of nurses and physicians: "Their profession calls for them to be guardians and servants of human life."[6] The encyclical notes that human life must be especially reverenced when it is most fragile: "the word of God frequently repeats the call to show care and respect, above all where life is undermined by sickness and old age."[7]

The Gospel of Life also addresses the health care settings in which many nurses practice: "...hospitals, clinics, and convalescent homes...should not merely be institutions where care is provided for the sick or the dying. Above all they should be places where suffering, pain and death are acknowledged and understood in their human and specifically Christian meaning."[8] Suffering is viewed in terms of "the salvific nature of the offering up of suffering which, experienced in communion with Christ, belongs to the very essence of the redemption"; and death is envisioned as "anything but an event without hope. It is the door which opens wide on eternity, and for those who live in Christ, an experience of participation in the mystery of his death and resurrection"[9] In a commentary on living according to the principles espoused in *The Gospel of Life,* the American Catholic bishops taught that physicians and nurses "...should be conscious evangelizers of their own professions, witnessing by word and example that God is the Lord of Life."[10]

In a dissertation exploring the relationship between reverence and the humanity of man, Mother Mary Aidan observed that "true reverence can only blossom out from a deep-rooted sense of God and the dignity of his creatures."[11] Christ was the "perfect exemplar of reverence during his life on earth," Mother Mary Aidan asserted; he taught reverence for each human person in parables like the Lost Sheep and the Prodigal Son.[12] Mother concluded that "as the vision of Christ in our brother grows, our reverence for our brother is increased until every contact with him is beautified with a divine graciousness."[13] Each of us, in following Jesus' commandment to love, should understand a brother or sister as "another self."[14] And, ultimately, as Albert Schweitzer reminded us, "reverence for life comprises the whole ethic of love in its deepest and highest sense. It is the source of constant renewal for the individual and for mankind."[15]

Nursing's Heritage of Reverence

Three identified characteristics of reverence that have meaning for practicing nurses include: *presence,* that is, a closeness to the one reverenced; *cherishing* or a love of appreciation; and *persuasion,* an active respect that supports the attainment of an individual's ultimate goals.[16] In examining the spiritual heritage of nursing one finds vivid examples of these characteristics in the lives and ministries of many of our Christian forebears.

The deacons and deaconesses serving in the first centuries A.D. exemplified *presence* for sick brothers and sisters, not only by visiting them where they lived, but also by taking the ill into their own homes, designating a space for the sick person that was labeled a "Christroom."[17] Early monastic nurses, such as Brigid of Ireland and Hilda of Whitby, *cherished* the sick, especially those afflicted with leprosy, treating them with tenderness and reverence and seeing in each patient the visage of the suffering Christ. Medieval monks and tertiaries continued this commitment to reverent care of the sick; one such was Francis of Assisi, distinguished for his gentle and loving care of lepers. And *persuasive* care for the souls as well as the bodies of the sick was evidenced by such figures as Catherine of Siena, patroness of nursing. During the plague epidemic of the fourteenth century Catherine is described as walking "night and day in the wards," praying with patients and helping them to find Christian hope and meaning in their suffering.[18] The post-Reformation period also provides a rich heritage of reverent care of the sick carried out by women religious nurses such as the Daughters of Charity, the Sisters of Mercy and the Kaiserswerth Deaconesses.[19] These sister nurses were deeply concerned with the spiritual as well as the physical well-being of those for whom they cared.

In exploring nursing's more recent history, from the early to the mid-twentieth century, numerous conceptualizations of reverence in caregiving are found in the literature. One poignant example is a metaphorical piece entitled "The Nurse's Mass," published in the December 1953 issue of *The Catholic Nurse*. The meditation begins: "'I will go unto the altar of God,' an altar on which Christ suffers and dies, an altar of white, a hospital bed."[20] The metaphor continues, identifying the nurse's uniform with priestly vestments and the patient's physical person with the chalice containing the body and blood of Jesus. The anonymous nurse-author notes, "I have been given the honor of ministering to His needs."[21] The conceptualization of the nurse's Mass concludes with the admission that while there may be no blessed candle or sanctuary lamp in a patient's room, the light of Christ shines within the nurse's heart, and gratitude is expressed for the gift of being allowed to minister to the sick and the afflicted in his name.[22]

In another early issue of *The Catholic Nurse*, Mother M. Virginia identified a vocation of reverence in describing the nurse as one who ministers to "the needs of the sick in both body and soul" in an "unobtrusive and sacred way."[23] And in a midcentury address to nurses Pope Pius XII acknowledged the challenge such ministry may at times pose for caregivers in his admonition to have reverence for the sick person who "at times loses much of what makes the human person respectable: courage, serenity and clearness."[24] The Holy Father advised, however, that the nurse must have "respect...for the temple of the Holy Spirit, redeemed by the precious blood of Christ, and destined for resurrection and eternal life."[25]

Contemporary nursing literature also documents incidents of reverence, especially those occurring at the time of a patient's birth or death. The birth of a child evokes reverence for many nurses: "The sense you get at a child's birth is the wonder of life, its mystery, its fragility and dependence, the responsibility you feel, the gentleness you know is inside you...."[26] And, in an article entitled simply "Reverence," nurse Anne Perry describes her experience with a terminally ill renal failure patient. Although not using the specific label, Perry likens her role in the death experience to that of a midwife.[27] (Several recent nursing publications have identified a conceptualization of "midwifing the dying."[28])[29] Perry reports: "For one magnificent moment I was there to hand her [the patient] off. Suspended in time and place the three of us touched: my patient, the one who came for her and me."[30]

Reverence for the patient after death, as a dimension of reverence for life, was also a topic explored in an issue of *Nursing Forum*. In discussing reverence for the dead, Jeanine Young-Mason employs Sophocles' *Antigone* as a model for the importance of providing for a patient's burial and preburial needs. The author cautions that "Without Antigone's honor and reverence for the dead, the human body can be objectified and desecrated,[31] and concludes by advising nurses to exercise ultimate reverence in caring for the deceased.[32]

Reverence in Definitions of Nursing

From the inception of the profession of nursing, reverence for the sacredness of human life has been understood, if not specifically named, in definitions of practice. In the mid-nineteenth-century Florence Nightingale strongly asserted her belief in reverence for the "living body" as a core concept of nursing:

> *Nursing is an art, and if it is to be made an art, it requires as exclusive a devotion, as hard a preparation, as any painter's or sculptor's work. For what is having to do with dead canvas or cold marble compared with having to do with the living body, the temple of God's spirit.*[33]

This attitude of considering reverence for life as central to the practice of nursing has progressed historically to the present day. During the first half of the twentieth century nurse-historians, such as Minnie Goodnow, presented the profession as a calling to provide reverent service to humanity.[34] In the 1950s nurse-author Alice Price offered a definition of nursing that included reverence for the patient's spiritual nature.[35] And in an article entitled: "Comforters of the Afflicted," published in a 1961 issue of *The Catholic Nurse*, Richard Cardinal Cushing, archbishop of Boston, warned nurses against being caught up in the technology of the day lest they lose their focus on reverence for life. His Eminence questioned: "Are we so concerned with treating diseases, and with treatments that new research develops, that we lose sight of the humanity of the patient?...Are we to close our eyes to the spark of divinity which glimmers behind the ailing body?"[36]

In the 1970s theorist Faye Abdellah articulated "criterion measures of patient care" that presumed reverence for life by including a component described as facilitating the patient's "achievement of personal spiritual goals."[37] In the 1980s Verna Benner Carson's definition of nursing accomplished a similar goal. Carson explained that the art of nursing includes a conscious decision to "serve" others; thus, she argues, even the simplest task "becomes a way of...touching the very core of [a client's] spirit."[38]

In the process of exploring the concepts of spirituality and healing in patients experiencing critical illness, contemporary author Kathryn Bizek asserted that spiritual care must include "reverence for life."[39] Similarly, in their clinical rotation handbook, nurses Marlene Reimer, Barbara Tomlison and Cathryn Bradshaw remind us that all patients "care and want to be cared for with the respect and dignity due them as human beings, regardless of their current state."[40] They add: "Never for a moment can that be forgotten, whether [he or she is] a physically aggressive nursing home resident...a severely deformed premature infant, or a brain dead patient whose organs are about to be transplanted."[41]

Judith Shelly and Arlene Miller, who have recently identified a Christian theology of nursing, presume reverence in practice by observing that "The role of the nurse...grew out of a Christian understanding of the human person as created in the image of God"; the body was viewed as a "temple of the Holy Spirit."[42]

Reverence in Clinical Practice

In order to understand more fully what reverence means to current practitioners, I interviewed twenty-five practicing nurses; fifteen were prepared at the baccalaureate level; ten had master's degrees in nursing. The comments of one MSN-prepared nurse working in an emergency room validated the earlier noted concept of reverence for the dead:

> Emergency room nurses will not give up bathing patients after they die. They'll stop what they're doing, even if they're really busy, and say: "I'm going to clean that person up before they (the mortuary) come for him." I think it's like the women who came to anoint Jesus' body after his death. Preparing the body is having reverence for who that person was in life and now in death. It's definitely nursing reverence.

Five key characteristics of reverence that emerged from analysis of the data reflecting the nurses' perceptions and clinical experiences included: *sacredness, respect, intimacy, caring* and *service.*

Sacredness
After God brought the Israelites out of Egypt, he said to Moses, who was encamped at Mt. Sinai with his people: "For the glorious adornment of your brother...you shall have *sacred* vestments made" (Exodus 28:2, emphasis added). The term *sacred* refers to something holy or religious, usually related to God or to a deity; to some aspect of transcendence. The Lord described the Israelite priest's vestments as *sacred*

in order to reflect their importance in designating participation in his service. It is noted that "the garments were intended to give [a person] dignity and honor not on his own account but as befits the one he serves and represents."[43] *Sacredness,* as a reflection of God's love and transcendence, is central to the concept of reverence for human life.

A master's-prepared maternal-child nurse, Mary, described the *sacredness* of reverence as making the concept "deeper than just respect":

> Respect is a part of reverence; respect is a graciousness, a kindness to people's differences, but reverence is feeling a real *sacredness* for human life. Reverence goes beyond respect and has to do with God; it is higher than respect.

As a clinical exemplar of reverence, Mary identified her work with multihandicapped children:

> These children, the quality of some of their lives is very poor. But you can reverence these children; it's not just respecting them, it's loving them. It's caring for them and seeing them as souls and children of God and not as somebody who shouldn't have been born, that there is meaning to their lives. There is a *sacredness* to their lives.

Another master's-prepared nurse, Gerrie, who had worked extensively with chronic renal-failure patients, reported that when caring for very ill patients she tried to see in them the "body of Christ": "It's like trying to recall to yourself the presence of God, internally." Gerrie gave an example:

> I remember one time, I had like hardly any time for prayer, and I was taking care of this woman who was dying. She had all the wounds of Christ on her. It was Holy Thursday and I didn't know how I could get to Mass but then when I was wiping her feet I thought of seeing Christ right there in the hospital bed. That's the *sacredness* of reverence; reverence for the patient; reverence for Christ within that patient.

Gerrie added: "It's in those transcendent moments, those sacred moments, that you see reverence more clearly."

Respect

The word *respect* means to have a high esteem or sense of awe in one's attitude toward a person or a thing. Saint Paul, in his Letter to the Romans, admonished his followers that they must "pay...respect to whom respect is due" (13:7). Because of the dignity of the human person, as God's creation, because of the sacredness of human life, all individuals deserve *respect*. It is a concept deeply embedded in the construct of *reverence;* it is a concept central to the practice of Christian nursing.

Jessica, a lieutenant commander in the U.S. Navy Nurse Corps, shared a touching example of *respect* for a soldier's life, which she recalled from her days of combat field nursing:

> I had this experience when I was a brand-new ensign in the Navy; it was during "Desert Storm" in the Persian Gulf. I was charge nurse in the ICU in a small field hospital about twenty miles from the Kuaiti boarder. One day they brought in a young soldier; he was only twenty-four years old and he was a UAE (United Arab Emirate) soldier. He had stepped on a land mine and both his legs were blown off, plus a lot of neuro damage as well. They did take him to surgery but there was nothing they could do, so they brought him to us to die. Looking at him, he was not of our faith, not of our culture, not of our military; he was an Arab soldier, but he was on our side. And it became evident that he was not going to make it and we—there were some young corpsmen in the ICU—didn't want him to die alone. So we went through his things to know his name, and we looked at a picture of his family, the people he loved, so that he wouldn't die alone. So there would be people with him who knew him and his family when he died. I remember looking at his family picture and thinking, "This is who this soldier is; these are the people who are important to him." And there was a reverence there, a *respect* for who the soldier was and

his life. Looking at him and respecting him as a person who was made by God; it was reverence for his life.

Intimacy

A synonym sometimes used to replace the term *intimacy* is *friendship*. *Friendship* may be defined as "the mutual good will of two persons who accept each other profoundly."[44] Driscoll adds that "The greatest form of friendship is the one established between God and humankind."[45] And Psalm 25:14 asserts: "The friendship of the Lord is with those who revere him." In order for friendship between two persons, or with the Lord, to occur, there must be a sense of *reverent intimacy* undergirding the relationship. A sense of reverent intimacy for those who were marginalized was modeled by the Jesus of Luke's gospel: "Shepherds instead of Magi came to his crib (2:8–18); he welcomed the sinful but penitent woman at a Pharisee's meal (7:30–50); he spoke well of Samaritans (10: 30-37); and he [sought] hospitality from a tax collector (19:1–10)."[46]

Sarah, a nurse working with the terminally ill, shared her perception that a reverent intimacy with patients becomes even more important when they are vulnerable:

> The nurse has to be so sensitive to the spiritual, to the reverence needs of sick people because they are so fragile. To be reverent of another is to respect the whole of them and to respect the fact that when you are invited into their lives it is a very *intimate* thing. You must be reverent because you are approaching more than a person's body, you are approaching their spirit as well; especially when it is a sick or disabled person. Certainly there is respect in reverence, but there is *intimacy* as well. The intimacy relates to the fact that reverence is a deeper phenomena that comes from relating to the spiritual dimension of the other person.

Cathy, a clinic nurse, explained her understanding of *intimacy* as a dimension of reverence, as related to physical touch:

I really do think that touching a patient is very *intimate* and needs to be very reverent. If a patient is going through an exam that is very frightening and a nurse holds her hand, that might be the thing that gets her through. It's intimate and it's reverence for her in her fear and her anxiety—who she is as a person with all her needs. I don't think nurses should ever get away from doing things like that; not if we're going to keep our sense of reverence for life.

Caring

"I was...ill and you cared for me."
Matthew 25:35–36

From this classic quotation recorded by the evangelist Matthew and supported by the parable of the Good Samaritan (Luke 10:30–37), I identified a nursing theology of caring that includes the concepts of: *being, listening* and *touching.*[47] Sometimes, during the darkest hours, when a patient is unable to speak about a painful problem, simply the caring presence, the *being with,* of a nurse provides enormous support. Margaret, a terminally ill oncology patient, described her best nurses as "the ones who sit with me and hold my hand when I'm too scared to talk." If, however, a patient or family member needs to speak about a fear or anxiety, the caring nurse *listens* with her heart as well as her ears and her mind. She listens with *reverence.* Finally, the caring nurse demonstrates *reverence* with her *touch,* whether physical or emotional. During instances of intense suffering the *reverent touch* of a loving nurse can bring solace and strength to patients and families, and a sense of joy and satisfaction to the nurse as well. Jesus taught us that "whatever you do for one of these least brothers of mine, you do for me" (Matthew 25:40). Scripture scholar Daniel Harrington observes that such deeds "deserve a reward at the last judgment because of the relationship of identity between the Son of Man and 'the least.'"[48]

"If we really *care*, if we have reverence for life in our hearts, it will show in our practice," commented Martha, a medical-surgical staff nurse. She added:

> I think what is important is that we are all clear about our mission to *care*, to be reverent. Everyone, no matter who they are, are God's creation, and we need to share and understand purely that we can support each other and care for each other. That kind of *caring* is reverence for the sacredness of all human life.

Ann, a psychiatric–mental health nursing instructor, related caring and reverence to seeing Christ in all of her patients:

> Reverence to me means *caring* for all people as the body of Christ. Early on in my nursing career I was always told to look at Christ, look at the person of Christ in whoever I met, in whoever I cared for. And so, to have reverence in nursing care I think of the Eucharist. It's like the reverence I have for the Eucharist should be reflected in my reverence when I give nursing care; really caring is that reverence.

Service

Jesus said to his disciples: *"Whoever wishes to be great among you will be your servant; whoever wishes to be first among you will be the slave of all. For the Son of Man did not come to be served but to serve and to give his life as a ransom for many"* (Mark 10:44–45).

In the Old Testament, righteous persons who belonged to God, such as Abraham, Isaac and Jacob were identified as being "servants," or in the service of the Lord.[49] In discussing the New Testament roots of service or *diaconia*, Helen Doohan notes that "Jesus presents an astonishing model of service...in washing his disciples' feet and serving at table."[50] For Saint Paul, Christian service to one's neighbor was considered as "service to Christ himself."[51] The person who "wants to follow the Son of Man must take an uncompromising stance against such non-gospel values as 'lording it over others.' To be a Christian is to be a servant as Jesus was."[52]

Ann, the psychiatric–mental health nurse quoted above, spoke also of service as a component of reverence and a dimension of caring. She described a clinical project carried out by some of her students working with homeless women:

> The students asked me if they could do something on foot care; the homeless have a lot of foot ulcers. And as the students were giving the foot care to the women and teaching them, you could just feel the reverence. It was the *service* component of the teaching project. I decided to participate myself, and it made me think of the Last Supper...[on] Holy Thursday: "as Christ did, so you also should do."

Ann concluded: "At postconference we talked about serving and about being reverent and about the scriptural reference for what we were doing. That's the reverence that I think we should all bring to our service as nurses."

Finally, Megan, an intensive care unit nurse explained her perception of service as a critical dimension of reverence:

> Reverence is a stance that I would try to take with any patient who comes to me. It's not my terrain or turf; it's about their need. I am there absolutely to *serve* them. I think serving with reverence should be my whole stance, my whole perspective, emotionally, psychologically, spiritually, that I should go before that patient and that family with. Not just whether they are behaving in a way that I approve of. It is respecting that they are...[children] of God in this or that stage of...life, with their own backgrounds and living in the circumstances they live in.

Megan concluded: "I think *service*, reverent service, is listening with your heart and putting it all together, like just being totally open to the person; I think reverence is a totally spiritual thing."

Nursing's Call to Reverence

From our earliest experiences as young students, nurses are imbued with a sense of reverence for the sacredness of human life. Who can not remember the absolute awe with which we assisted in the delivery room for the first time: the excitement, and sense of amazement we felt as we heard a perfect tiny human person cry out and fill his or her lungs with air to signal the beginning of life in this world? And who of us, also, can ever forget the poignancy of the first time we assisted at the bedside of a dying patient? We experienced a different kind of awe and wonder, tinged perhaps now with human sadness, as we were gifted to witness the end of life and a birth into eternity. All along the continuum of human existence, from the birthing to the dying experience, nurses are graced, as Florence Nightingale taught, by the blessing of deep intimacy with "God's precious gift of life." No other profession provides the opportunity to touch and be touched by the human spirit as does the practice of nursing. It is this intimacy that calls us to reverence: reverence for God as our creator and Lord; reverence for those blessed with the sacredness of human life; and reverence for our nursing practice as a vocation of service to brothers and sisters in need.

CHAPTER 8.
IN THE POTTER'S HANDS:

The Spirituality of Nursing

"Indeed, like clay in the hand of the potter, so are you in my hand."
—*Jeremiah 18:6*

Nurses like to be in control. That's not meant to be a pejorative statement. It's simply the way most of us have been trained. We are educated to be on top of the situation, whether managing, teaching, researching or caring for patients. As Florence Nightingale reminded us, often patients' lives are "literally placed in [the nurse's] hands."[1] Being in control doesn't mean that we don't try to understand the personal concerns of those for whom we care; actually our listening presence is all part of the package of being in control. A *good* nurse might well be described as one who "has it all together" in whatever caregiving situation he or she functions. That includes sensitivity to the emotional needs and desires of patients and families as well as skilled physical care. While the nursing characteristic of *control* may be positive in the clinical setting, it can, however, be problematic in the spiritual realm.

Although I would prefer not to admit it, I like to be in control; it makes me feel secure. I am also aware that my desire to feel in control may take away an important element of trust in God's providence and his care. While I would surely never suggest that nurses abdicate responsibility for professional activities, a conscious awareness of God's caring presence and God's power will not only support our work but will relieve us of the unnecessary guilt related to our inability to accomplish the impossible.

The Potter's Hands

Because of my penchant for control, one of my favorite scripture passages is the anecdote described in the Book of Jeremiah the prophet, chapter 18, verses 1 through 6. It's the Old Testament story of how God spoke to Jeremiah, advising him to go and visit the house of a local potter. God told the prophet to watch how the potter would take a lump of clay, which had not turned out well on his wheel, and remold the object so it would become what he wanted. Then the Lord reminded him that he, Jeremiah, as all of Israel, was in God's hands, *"like clay in the hands of the potter."*

In an introduction to the book of Jeremiah, Old Testament scholar Lawrence Boadt, C.S.P., notes that what emerges from reading the work is the image of a man who "saw the hand of God so clearly in the events of his day."[2] Because of this, Father Boadt observes, "Jeremiah was recognized by his own contemporaries as a prophet whose words were worth saving and handing on, and even expanding and reusing in new situations of danger and discouragement."[3]

The symbolism of Jeremiah's visit to the potter has been described by numerous Old Testament scholars. The image of Yahweh as potter expresses the "absolute dependence of man on God in the order of creation."[4] The metaphor of the

potter controlling the clay by manipulating his wheel represents him as the "master of what he will create."[5] While the
narrative depicts God's "freedom" of interaction with those
he created,[6] it also illustrates the fact that God, as Creator of
humankind, "knew what sort of man" he had produced,
"how [he] would act," and God's response.[7] As the church
father Origen mused: "God, the potter of our body...when
this has fallen and been crushed...can take it up and renew it
and make it beautiful and better...pleasing in his view."[8] Jeremiah speaks, in the potter's-house narrative, not only to those
who lived in the sixth century B.C., "but to all who consent to
the process of the pilgrimage....The spoiled vase is rework-
able, and the old clay can be molded into a new creation."[9]
"God never abandons his clay," Carlo Carretto asserts: "What
crackings; what botchings! But God keeps remaking the mix-
ture; he never gives up."[10]

Whenever I read the Jeremiah story, instead of "Jeremiah"
I put my own name into the narrative. This helps remind me
that I, as Jeremiah, am asked to be *like clay in the hands of the
potter.*" And my prayer is that if I, in my desire for control, am
molding the clay of my life to become something other than
what God wishes, he will redirect my efforts in *whatever way
he pleases.* Perhaps as you read the Jeremiah passage below,
you might try a similar meditation. Enter into the narrative
and for a few minutes become Jeremiah; listen to God's loving voice as he speaks to your heart:

> *This word came to Jeremiah from the LORD: Rise up, be
> off to the potter's house; there I will give you my message. I
> went down to the potter's house and there he was, working
> at the wheel. Whenever the object of clay which he was
> making turned out badly in his hand, he tried again,
> making of the clay another object of whatever sort he
> pleased. Then the word of the LORD came to me: "Can I
> not do to you...as this potter has done says the LORD.
> Indeed, like clay in the hand of the potter, so are you in my
> hand."*
>
> Jeremiah 18:1–6

In meditating on Jeremiah's visit to the potter, ask yourself: Cannot God do with me *"as this potter has done?"*

The Spirituality of the Wheel

Cylindrical disks connected with an axle, which were originally designed for transportation purposes, were later adapted for such uses as the "potter's wheel for shaping the clay."[11] The potter's wheel has important spiritual symbolism. Its symbolic message relates especially to the submissive nature of the clay, which must lie in wait on the wheel to be molded by the master potter. A related metaphor, using the example of the sculptor's chisel, was advanced by seventeenth-century spiritual writer Jean-Pierre de Caussade, who imagined that the stone's response might be:

> *I know...I must stay immovable in the hands of the sculptor, and I must love him and endure all he inflicts on me to produce the figure he has in mind....I have no idea what he is doing, nor do I know what he will make of me. But what I do know is that his work is the best possible.*[12]

Missionary Kay Wagoner described such an experience in a *Journal of Christian Nursing* article entitled: "A Nurse's Spin on the Potter's Wheel."[13] Nurse Wagoner admitted to encountering numerous difficulties in attempting to practice and minister in a European country whose culture was unfamiliar. She explained, however, using the Jeremiah scripture, how the Lord used the experience to deepen her spirituality: "God, in his wisdom had broken me down and placed me on the potter's wheel and molded me into the person he wanted me to be."[14]

As I was writing these thoughts related to the Jeremiah scripture, I began to wish that I could find a picture of a potter's wheel. I wanted to better understand the creative process of working with clay, something I had never done. Instead, I met a potter! And I discovered that there was a wonderful "potter's house," called Salve Regina, right on my own university campus. The potter spoke to me of the artistry of molding clay and introduced me to the concepts of the *wheel,* the *glaze* and the *furnace.* A few weeks later I had the privilege of "going down to the potter's house," like Jeremiah, and watching a master potter "working at the wheel." I loved the ambiance of the airy, dusty room cluttered with emerging earthen pots in various stages of completion. The potter's workspace was of a classic style. It was comprised of a wooden frame, actually two wooden benches: one for the potter to sit on and the other supporting the top half of the wheel on which the clay would be formed. Close to the floor was the bottom disk of the wheel, connected by a metal shaft to the top. This cylinder, called the kick wheel, is moved by the potter's foot and turns the molding wheel above. I was told that some art studios have now adopted modern mechanized potter's wheels; I'm glad my university's art department has not. The traditional foot-operated wheel seems so reminiscent of biblical times and of the spiritual meaning of the creative molding of the clay.

As I watched the contemporary master potter, I noticed that he compressed the clay several times with his hands before placing it on the wheel. This process, he explained, removed any air pockets and kept the ingredients consistent, making the clay stronger. After the compressed lump of clay was "thrown" on the quickly spinning wheel, the potter again used his hands in a variety of movements to guide the evolution of the emerging piece of pottery. It took significant strength and skill for him to repeatedly reshape and "center" the clay before the pot was completed. This action of centering, the potter described poetically as *"the dance of molding the clay";* as the potter's hands pressed down, the clay rose up to begin forming the walls of the vessel. If, he observed, too little pressure is used in the centering, nothing happens to the clay; if too much is used, the pot breaks.

The master potter admitted that, before beginning to work at the wheel, he envisions "rather specifically" how he wants a piece to turn out. When I noticed that his hands became coated with the wet clay he was working, the potter mused that a kind of interaction occurs between the clay and the potter as part of the *"dance of the molding."*

My "Jeremiah" experience of watching the potter working at his wheel provided a number of new metaphors for a nurse's spirituality. The activity of compressing the clay to purify and strengthen it reminded me that God, our Master Potter, sometimes needs to apply some spiritual pressure to cleanse our hearts and prepare them to hear the voice of his Spirit. In these actions God, our Father, uses power and artistry to guide our walk with him. Also, the contemporary potter's use of the term *centering* to describe his "dance of molding the clay" struck me as analogous to the concept of centering our lives and our hearts in prayer. In this way one's spirit is opened to experience God's loving presence, to allow the Lord to draw us to himself and to make our hearts like unto his own—to become his instruments in the service of the sick. God, the Master Potter of our souls, knows exactly how much pressure we need to grow spiritually; he will never exert more than we are able to bear.

After skillfully turning out several lovely clay vessels, my contemporary potter suggested that I try my hand at the wheel. It looked so easy that I agreed. Needless to say I quickly discovered that I am no master potter. I was left, after several rather frustrating attempts, with only an amorphous looking blob of unmolded clay sitting in the middle of my wheel. And, I had to think that perhaps that is precisely what happens to my plans when I try to take control away from God. Whenever I foolishly decide that I must be in charge of what should happen next, things seem to have a way of ending up like the sad little lump of unformed clay, woefully lacking the skilled and tender touch of the divine Master Potter of my spiritual journey.

Ultimately, a pottery wheel carries the clay round and round in continually moving circles as the master potter's hands gently yet firmly push and pull, molding the vessel into the final shape and form he envisions. There are days when we feel as if we were sitting, like clay, in the middle of a potter's wheel, going round and round, as the shape of our daily lives is moved and changed by some mysterious external force. Despite our faith-filled hopes and best-laid plans, things seem to be spinning out of control, at least out of our personal control. This can be a very frustrating experience. Just think of one of your best nursing horror stories, like the morning you came on duty to discover that five patients were scheduled for early-morning surgery; that the night shift had two codes, so no preoperative meds had been given; two staff nurses on the "seven to three shift" called in sick with the flu; that the unit clerk was on jury duty; and that JCAHO (the Joint Commission of American Hospital Organizations) was scheduled to visit your unit that day.

Now, I'm not about to propose that if you have faith, God will miraculously arrive on the floor to take charge of morning care or to get the O.R. patients prepped and off to surgery. God, our Father, our Holy Mystery, doesn't operate like that. But I am suggesting that, with faith, we can trust that his presence is continually resting within our hearts, waiting for a thought or a prayer. As any loving parent, he is ever vigilant over the problems of his children. God doesn't need long prayers, especially in situations like the one described above. If you are spinning around on an emotional potter's wheel, you won't have the time to wax eloquent in your praying. That's OK. It's not fancy words but just our hearts and our love that God is waiting for. The simple pilgrim's prayer, "Come, Lord Jesus," will do fine. The Lord only wants to know that we know he's around. And if you've got a tough decision to make, you might try the brief mantra that a spiritual director once taught me: "Lord lead me; Lord guide me; Lord show me the way."

Although the feeling of spinning around on a potter's wheel is not a pleasant experience, it may be exactly the kind of spiritual exercise that the Lord can use to begin the process of molding us in his loving image. He alone knows the shape and the form he would have us assume in the practice of our nursing. The challenge for us is to accept and to welcome the gentle embrace of the *Potter's hands.*

Glazing the Clay

The Hiddenness of Nursing

Clay is a substance made of earth and water; it is pliable when soft yet hardens into a solid mass when allowed to dry or when baked in a fire. Two distinctive characteristics of clay are the fact that it can be molded into a "particular shape"; and when fired to temperatures as high as 700 to 900 degrees fahrenheit, it becomes "almost impervious to decay or corrosion."[15] The clay can, however, be broken or shattered by strong force or impact.[16] One of the earliest uses of clay was for the making of pottery.[17]

How like we are, as nurses, to the above description of clay. Our personalities, our nursing personas, are "soft and pliable" when we are new to the profession; then we are formed and molded by our classes, our colleagues and our clinical experiences. We can and generally do take on a "particular shape" after we have been "fired" in the line of duty, following some years of practice. Our characters will, hopefully, become "impervious to decay" once they have been tested and tried by daily stresses. But we can also "be broken or shattered" if the impact of the sufferings related to our profession is too great. In the beginning of our nursing experience we are like raw clay; it is for the Master Potter to glaze and beautify the nurses we are to become.

Raw, moist clay, which has been prepared for molding either by hand or on a potter's wheel, retains a color somewhere between tan and reddish brown, depending upon the type of earth and the amount of water in the mix. A clay object that has been glazed and fired, however, may take on an entirely different color or colors, depending upon the type and amount of glaze used to coat the raw material. Basically, glazes are mineral compounds that coat the clay with a "thin layer of glass."[18] One of the potters I mentioned earlier gifted me with a small earthenware jar beautifully decorated in subtle shades of blue and gray, two of my favorite colors. She explained that ultimately the original clay becomes *hidden* as it were, overlaid with one or more of a variety of colored glazes. While the glazing technique can add beauty and a sense of richness to the molded piece, it is the power and the strength of the raw clay *hidden* underneath that is the essence of the completed vessel.

Thus, when the pottery comes out of the fire, its original appearance is obscured from the observer's view. It's the same, I think, with the nurse's spiritual journey. While some dimensions of her faith experience may be revealed during caregiving activities, much of a nurse's spirituality and spiritual presence remains hidden. This is the nature of transcendent Christian spirituality.

If, then, a nurse's spirituality is hidden, what in fact is meant by the words *spiritual presence?* As I understand the concept, spiritual presence refers to the faith-oriented stance or posture one assumes in interaction with others. In my earlier book exploring spirituality and nursing, I described the nurse's spiritual presence or spiritual posture as *standing on holy ground.*[19] To *stand on holy ground* means to stand before our sick brothers and sisters in the radiance of the Father's protecting light. To *stand on holy ground* means to be an earthen vessel filled with the tenderness of the Son's healing light. To *stand on holy ground* means to become a channel of understanding blessed with the wisdom of the spirit's energizing light. To *stand on holy ground* means to learn the art of personal hiddenness and to become an instrument of God's enfolding presence. He must increase; we must decrease. This is the hiddenness that reveals Jesus, the Light of the world; this is spiritual presence in nursing.

One evening, while listening to the happenings of the day being shared by a young sister-nurse with whom I was living, I was struck by the personal hiddenness of her work with frail nursing home residents. Sister Ann expressed delight at the elders' small joys on such occasions as a visit with a family member or the celebration of a birthday. She also empathized tenderly with the pains of those whose physical and cognitive abilities seemed to be decreasing by leaps and bounds. What touched me, especially, was the fact that, because of their frailty, a great number of Sister Ann's patients were severely limited in their ability to respond to her ministrations. Many were not capable of providing the heartwarming smile or word of thanks that can provide a nurse the strength to keep going no matter how tired or frustrated she might feel.

There are not a whole lot of accolades given, even within our own profession, for weeks, months or sometimes years of dedicated service in the field of long-term care. Geriatric nurses are some of our members who truly practice, as nurse historian Patricia Donahue would put it, the "finest art";[20] yet it is also often a hidden art. Sister Ann's dedication to gentle care and compassion, frequently carried out behind the closed door of the patient's room, is an example of such *hidden* art at its finest. The professional image of Sister Ann capably managing a nursing unit housing peaceful, well-cared-for patients is the external beauty of the colorfully glazed pot; the raw clay *hidden* underneath is Sister's day-to-day commitment and care in the midst of difficult and sometimes soul-wearying nursing activities. The world sees Sister Ann's *glaze;* God sees and blesses the *hiddenness* of her secret struggles. The Master Potter sees and blesses her spiritual presence in nursing.

The Furnace

One of the things that especially fascinated me about the making of pottery was the process of firing the clay: baking the molded pot, at high temperatures, in a furnace or kiln. The higher the kiln temperature achieved, the harder the pottery becomes. My master potter reaffirmed that a pottery vessel is formed by the person making it, and that includes his or her control of the fire. He asserted, "The potter needs a sensitivity to the clay so as not to fire a piece too high to cause it to break." Nevertheless, there is always a risk when working with the fire.

When another potter showed me one of her creations that had broken in half during the firing, I commented sympathetically; "What a shame!" "Oh, no!" she exclaimed, "That's the risk you take; you have to take a chance on a piece being broken when it goes into the furnace. You have to be able to let go when you put something into the fire." She added: "There's a lot of uncertainty in this art; you can't be someone who needs a sure thing if you do pottery. What comes out of the fire is always a surprise." More wonderful metaphors, I thought, for nurses' spiritual journeys, especially in relation to some of our challenging clinical experiences, when we feel that we have indeed been through a fiery furnace in our ministry of caring for God's fragile ones.

The term *fire* has important biblical significance. While it may sometimes be symbolic of destruction, it can also be understood as a purging or purifying "metaphor of God's holiness."[21] In the first letter of Saint Peter such a metaphor was used to encourage the early Christians who were experiencing myriad difficulties:

> *In this you rejoice, although now for a little while you may have to suffer through various trials, so that the genuineness of your faith, more precious than gold that is perishable even though tested by fire, may prove to be for praise, glory, and honor at the revelation of Jesus Christ.*
>
> 1 Peter 1:6–7

The meaning of the word *furnace* as a receptacle for fire is used in the Bible to metaphorically describe "God's presence" and the "redemption of his people."[22] The prophet Isaiah recorded God's message: "See, I have refined you like silver, tested you in the *furnace* of affliction" (48:10, emphasis added).

The concept of a furnace as God's purifying instrument on our spiritual journey is poignantly described by Hannah Hurnard in her allegory *Hind's Feet on High Places* (also referred to in chapter four). In one portion of the narrative the Chief Shepherd explains to his follower Much Afraid: "All of my servants on their way to the high places have had to make this detour through the desert. It is called the *furnace* of Egypt....Here they have learned many things which otherwise they would have known nothing about."[23] In the following pages of Hurnard's allegory the Shepherd demonstrates for Much Afraid how rough pieces of stone, having been fired in the *furnace*, come out resembling beautiful jewels. The Shepherd then observes:

"My rarest and choicest jewels and my finest gold are those who have been refined in the *furnace* of Egypt," and he sings one verse of a little song: "I'll turn my hands upon thy heart, and purge away the dross, I will refine thee in my *fire*, remake thee at my Cross."[24]

And it is, of course, precisely the message of the cross to which the Good Shepherd, the Lord Jesus, is leading the Christian nurse. For it is only at the foot of his cross that we shall find our hope; it is at the foot of his cross that we shall regain our strength; and it is at the foot of his cross that we shall feel our joy, even as we witness daily the pain and suffering so central to our ministry of nursing the sick.

I'm always deeply touched by nurses' descriptions of their patients' trials. I can hear the pain in a nurse's voice, see the sorrow in a nurse's eyes and feel the empathy in a nurse's soul as she attempts to cross over and stand with her patient in that place of sickness where the ill person is alone and afraid. As noted in chapter six, the nurse, like Simon of Cyrene, is often asked to assist her patients in carrying their crosses; she is asked to share with them the searing heat of the fire—and of the furnace. This can be both a challenge and a grace. I remember once accompanying a patient/friend to the O.R. for radical surgery. As we moved her onto the surgical gurney, she looked at me with tears in her eyes and whispered, so only I could hear, "I'm so scared." I thought my heart would break. My patient and my friend was on her way to the *fire*, and as I walked along beside her O.R. cart I felt as if I was going into that *furnace* right along with her. In order to fill up the waiting time I had brought along a briefcase full of papers, a mountain of work to be accomplished during the procedure. Instead, I paced the halls and watched the hands of the clock move until the surgery was successfully over. I experienced, I think, a nurse's *furnace* that afternoon.

As well as sharing in the pain of patients' suffering, we may also have to cope with personal *furnace* times; problems and concerns of our own that must be kept hidden during the carrying out of nursing activities. Such stressors as the illness of a family member or the support needs of a close friend must be relegated to the back burner of our consciousness during work hours, so that competent and caring attention will be given to those in our charge. This is not an easy thing to do. It reminds me again of Henri Nouwen's concept of the wounded healer, which was discussed in chapter four. Nouwen, in exploring the loneliness of the minister, essentially raises the question of who ministers to the minister.[25] We might add to such a discussion the query: Who cares for the caregiver? Or more specifically, who provides nursing for the nurse? Our answer of course must be he, alone, who bears us up on "eagles' wings" (Isaiah 40:31), who has written our names "upon the palms of [his] hands" (Isaiah 49:16) and who will not allow our "foot to slip" (Psalm 121:3).

And so it continues, from day to day, this spiritual journey to which all nurses are called. We move from the potter's wheel, to the hiddenness beneath our professional glaze, to the fiery furnace in which, God willing, our spirituality is refined and burnished. Our prayer, in the end, is that we may become the earthen pot that the Lord would have us become, God's vessel into which his love is poured and from which his love is outpoured to those we are privileged to serve.

God's Vessel

The Nurse's Spirituality

The Old Testament scriptures remind us repeatedly that we are God's own vessels in such passages as Genesis 2:7: *"The* LORD *God formed man out of the clay of the ground and blew into his nostrils the breath of life, and so man became a living being"*;
and Isaiah 64:7: *"Yet, O* LORD, *you are our father;/ we are clay and you the potter: we are all the work of your hands."*

Some of the synonyms for the word *vessel* include: "*hollow* utensil," "container," "receptacle," "jar," "pot," "bowl," and "chalice";[26] early pottery vessels were used primarily for "storage and transportation."[27] Ideally any vessel is constructed of material strong and sturdy enough to be filled with another substance and not to break or crack while being used. In order for a potter to create a durable earthen vessel, he must know how to find "the right raw materials and...the best method of...shaping, decorating and firing the ware."[28]

The nurse, as God's spiritual vessel, needs also to have a *hollow* place in her heart; an empty place for the Lord to fill with his own love and his tenderness. This place may then become a wellspring of compassion for her suffering patients. God, the Master Potter, created the *raw materials* of the nurse's spiritual journey, and he alone knows the best method of *shaping, decorating* and *firing* her spirituality. One of the contemporary potters with whom I spoke explained that, in using the wheel, there is a "rhythm to the work....At times," she commented, "if the clay is heavy, the wheel is moved fast; but it may also be turned very slowly if the shaping is delicate." Sometimes our spiritual journey seems like that. There are days when it is filled with excitement, moving along at a very rapid pace—times when we have experienced a wonderful retreat or period of prayer, or when we have found just the right spiritual book that touches the heart and lifts the spirit. At other times the rhythm of our walk with God goes more gently, even on occasion, seeming to come to a complete standstill, and we wonder if we have lost our way. But we need not fear. The Master Potter who has asked us to be as *clay in his hands,* will never abandon us. Although we may have dark days, the *furnace* experiences, these are also held in the Father's hands as he *fires* and strengthens us to become the vessel he desires.

Henri Nouwen introduced a paradigm of how God forms each of us spiritually; he asserted that, in God's loving plan, we are "chosen," "blessed," "broken" and "given" to those around us.[29] When I read Father Nouwen's words, I find myself very attracted to three of those concepts:

Chosen—Who would not want to perceive themselves as one of God's own?

Blessed—What a joy to be anointed by the Lord!

Given—It is a reward in itself to be God's gift to those one wishes to serve.

The problem, for me, in Henri Nouwen's schema, however, is that immediately before the grace of being given, there resides the requirement that one be broken. And the thought of being broken is not something that particularly captures my heart; in fact it frightens me a great deal. To recognize oneself as broken, as shattered, as cracked is to risk losing control: losing control over the secure and safe image of self that society mandates as so essential to our lives. Control is viewed as especially necessary to functioning in a professional arena such as that of nursing. And yet to be broken, to be vulnerable, can put one in a wonderful place of being ready to let go of what is superfluous. We are forced to surrender those things that we thought essential to our material lives, and we become open to receive those things that God knows are critical to our spiritual lives.

Just as the clay pot needs the fire of the furnace to become a sturdy and beautiful earthen vessel, so we need the furnace of brokenness to make us into a spiritual vessel from which others may draw the "living waters" of Jesus' love. This is the heart of a nurse's spirituality; to become a strong but empty vessel, God's vessel, for him to fill and use as he chooses in the service of the ill and the infirm. To be *chosen and given* to the sick in his name is God's gift to us as nurses; we, among all persons, are most truly blessed.

NOTES

Chapter 1: A Cup of Cold Water

1. John Cardinal O'Connor, *A Moment of Grace: John Cardinal O'Connor On the Catechism of the Catholic Church* (San Francisco: Ignatius Press, 1995), 214.

2. Ibid.

3. Ibid.

4. Anne L. Austin, *History of Nursing Sourcebook* (New York: G. P. Putnam's Sons, 1957), 90.

5. Julia D. Emblen, "Religion and Spirituality Defined According to Current Use in Nursing Literature," *Journal of Professional Nursing* 8:1 (1992): 41–47, p. 41.

6. Ibid.

7. Jane Dyson, Mark Cobb and Dawn Forman, "The Meaning of Spirituality: A Literature Review," *Journal of Advanced Nursing* 26 (1997): 1183–88, p. 1183.

8. Bernice Golberg, "Connection: An Exploration of Spirituality in Nursing Care," *Journal of Advanced Nursing* 27 (1998): 836–42, p. 836.

9. Margaret Burkhardt, "Reintegrating Spirituality into Healthcare," *Alternative Therapies* 4:2 (1998): 127–28, p. 128.

10. Joann W. Conn, "Spirituality," in *The New Dictionary of Theology*, eds. Joseph Komonchak, Mary Collins and Dermot Lane (Collegeville, Minn.: Liturgical Press, 1990), 972–86, p. 972.

11. M. Patricia Donahue, *Nursing: The Finest Art,* 2nd ed. (St. Louis: Mosby-Yearbook, Inc., 1996), 2.

12. Margaret O. Doheny, Christina B. Cook and Mary C. Stopper, *The Discipline of Nursing: An Introduction,* 4th ed. (Stamford, Conn.: Appleton & Lange, 1997), 3.

13. Janice B. Lindberg, Mary L. Hunter and Ann Z. Kruszewski, *Introduction to Nursing: Concepts, Issues and Opportunities* (Philadelphia: Lippincott-Raven, 1998), 9.

14. J. Cheryl Exum, "Nurse," in *Harper's Bible Dictionary,* ed. Paul J. Achtemeier (New York: Harper & Row, 1985), 713–14, p. 714.

15. Daniel J. Harrington, *The Gospel According to Matthew* (Collegeville, Minn.: Liturgical Press, 1991), 49.

16. Phyllis A. Bird, "Water," in *Harper's Bible Dictionary,* ed. Paul J. Achtemeier (New York: Harper & Row, 1985), 1120–21, p. 1121.

17. Donald Senior and Pheme Perkins, "Introduction to the Synoptic Gospels," in The Catholic Study Bible, New American Bible, eds. Donald Senior, Mary Ann Getty, Carroll Stuhlmueller and John J. Collins (New York: Oxford University Press, 1990), 386RG–481RG, p. 396RG.

18. Mary Elizabeth O'Brien, *Spirituality in Nursing: Standing on Holy Ground* (Sudbury, Mass.: Jones and Bartlett, 1999), 85.

19. Ibid., 155.

20. Lawrence Boadt, *Reading the Old Testament: An Introduction* (Mahwah, N.J.: Paulist Press, 1984), 547.

21. Joseph G. Allegretti, *The Lawyer's Calling: Christian Faith and Legal Practice* (Mahwah, N.J.: Paulist Press, 1996), 21.

22. Philip A. Kalish and Beatrice J. Kalish, *The Advance of American Nursing* (Philadelphia: J. B. Lippincott, 1995), 117.

23. Sister M. Berenice Beck, *The Nurse: Handmaid of the Divine Physician* (Philadelphia: J. B. Lippincott, 1945), xvii.

24. Henri J. M. Nouwen, *Creative Ministry* (New York: Doubleday Image Books, 1991), 56.

25. Mary C. Cooper, "Covenantal Relationships: Grounding for the Nursing Ethic," *Advances in Nursing Science* 10:4 (1988): 48–59.

26. Carol L. Montgomery, "The Care-Giving Relationship: Paradoxical and Transcendent Aspects," *Alternative Therapies* 2:4 (1996): 52–57.

27. Daniel P. Sulmasy, *The Healer's Calling: A Spirituality for Physicians and Other Health Care Professionals* (Mahwah, N.J.: Paulist Press, 1997), 31.

28. Mary Elizabeth O'Brien, *The Courage to Survive: The Life Career of the Chronic Dialysis Patient* (New York: Grune & Stratton, 1983), 74.

29. M. Simone Roach, "Reflections on the Theme," in *Caring from the Heart: The Convergence of Caring and Spirituality*, ed. M. Simone Roach (Mahwah, N.J.: Paulist Press, 1997), 8.

30. Henri J. M. Nouwen, *Lifesigns: Intimacy, Fecundity and Ecstasy in Christian Perspective* (New York: Doubleday Image, 1989), 75.

31. Frank J. Matera, "Gospel," in *Harper's Bible Dictionary*, ed. Paul J. Achtemeier (New York: Harper & Row, 1985), 354–55, p. 354.

32. Elizabeth A. Livingstone, ed., *The Concise Oxford Dictionary of the Christian Church* (New York: Oxford University Press, 1990), 218.

33. Brother Roger of Taize, *His Love Is a Fire* (Collegeville, Minn.: Liturgical Press, 1990), 60.

CHAPTER 2: "IN EARTHEN VESSELS"

1. Mary Elizabeth O'Brien, *The AIDS Challenge: Breaking Through the Boundaries* (Westport, Conn.: Auburn House, 1995), 143.

2. Mary Elizabeth O'Brien, *Spirituality in Nursing: Standing On Holy Ground* (Sudbury, Mass.: Jones and Bartlett, 1999), 88.

3. Ibid., 100.

4. Thomas D. McGonigle, "Ministry," in *The New Dictionary of Catholic Spirituality*, ed. Michael Downey (Collegeville, Minn.: Liturgical Press, 1993), 658–59, p. 658.

5. Joyce Rupp, *May I Have This Dance?* (Notre Dame, Ind.: Ave Maria Press, 1993), 118.

6. Henri J. M. Nouwen, *The Genesee Diary: Report from a Trappist Monastery* (New York: Doubleday, 1989).

7. Brother Roger of Taize, *His Love Is a Fire* (Collegeville, Minn.: Liturgical Press, 1990), 62.

8. Phyllis A. Bird, "Vessel," in *Harper's Bible Dictionary,* ed. Paul J. Achtemeier (New York: Harper & Row, 1985), 1111.

9. Donald Senior, Mary Ann Getty, Carroll Stuhlmueller and John J. Collins, eds., The Catholic Study Bible: New American Bible (New York: Oxford University Press, 1990), New Testament: 281, note 4:7.

10. David Alexander and Pat Alexander, eds., *Eerdmans' Handbook to the Bible* (Grand Rapids, Mich.: William B. Eerdmans, 1992), 599.

11. John J. O'Rourke, "The Second Letter to the Corinthians," in *The Jerome Biblical Commentary,* eds. Raymond E. Brown, Joseph A. Fitzmyer and Roland Murphy (Englewood Cliffs, N.J.: Prentice-Hall, 1968), 280.

12. James L. Price, "The Second Letter to the Corinthians," in *The Interpreter's One-Volume Commentary on the Bible,* ed., Charles M. Laymon (Nashville, Tenn.: Abingdon, 1982), 813–23, p. 816.

13. William Barclay, *The Letter to the Corinthians,* rev. ed., (Philadelphia: Westminster Press, 1975), 197.

14. Donald Senior and Pheme Perkins "The Gospels and Acts," in The Catholic Study Bible: New American Bible, eds. Donald Senior, Mary Ann Getty, Carroll Stuhlmueller and John J. Collins (New York: Oxford University Press, 1990), RG386–RG469, p. RG393.

15. Daniel J. Harrington, *The Gospel According to Matthew* (Collegeville, Minn.: Liturgical Press, 1991), 24.

16. O'Brien, *The AIDS Challenge,* 140–41.

17. Elizabeth A. Livingstone, *The Concise Oxford Dictionary of the Christian Church* (New York: Oxford University Press, 1990), 67.

CHAPTER 3: "SOMEONE TOUCHED ME"

1. Edward J. Mally, "The Gospel According to Mark," in *The Jerome Biblical Commentary,* eds. Raymond E. Brown, Joseph A. Fitzmyer, and Roland Murphy (Englewood Cliffs, N.J.: Prentice-Hall, 1968), 2–36, p. 33.

2. Jerome Kodell, *The Gospel According to Luke* (Collegeville, Minn.: Liturgical Press, 1989), 51–52.

3. David Alexander and Pat Alexander, eds., *Eerdmans' Handbook to the Bible* (Grand Rapids, Mich.: William B. Eerdmans, 1992), 505.

4. Donald Senior, *Jesus: A Gospel Portrait* (Mahwah, N.J.: Paulist Press, 1992), 7.

5. J. Champlin, *Healing in the Catholic Church: Mending Wounded Hearts and Bodies* (Huntington, Ind.: Our Sunday Visitor, 1985), 35.

6. Edward Schillebeeckx, *Jesus, An Experiment in Christology*, Hubert Hoskins, trans. (New York: Seabury Press, 1979), 180.

7. Senior, 100–101.

8. Rene Latourelle, *The Miracles of Jesus and the Theology of the Miracles* (Mahwah, N.J. : Paulist Press, 1988), 4.

9. Alexander and Alexander, 480.

10. Kodell, 35.

11. Alexander and Alexander, 541–42.

12. Neal M. Flanagan, *The Gospel According to John and the Johannine Epistles* (Collegeville, Minn.: Liturgical Press, 1989), 45.

13. A. Weiser, *The Miracles of Jesus Then and Now* (New York: Franciscan Herald Press, 1972), 44.

14. Senior, 112.

15. Ibid.

16. Senior, 114–15.

17. Karl Rahner, *The Content of Faith* (New York: Crossroad, 1992).

18. Judith Allen Shelly, "Is Prayer Unprofessional?" (editorial), *Journal of Christian Nursing* 12:1 (1995): 3.

19. Sister Mary Berenice Beck, *The Nurse: Handmaid of the Divine Physician* (Philadelphia: J.B. Lippincott, 1945).

20. Daniel J. Harrington, *The Gospel According to Matthew* (Collegeville, Minn.: Liturgical Press, 1991), 37.

21. Constance H. Sumner, "Recognizing and Responding to Spiritual Distress," *American Journal of Nursing* 98:1 (1998): 26–31, p. 28.

22. Judith Allen Shelly and Sharon Fish, *Spiritual Care: The Nurse's Role* (Downer's Grove, Ill.: InterVarsity Press, 1988), 96.

23. Brother Roger of Taize, *His love Is a Fire* (Collegeville, Minn.: Liturgical Press, 1990), 65.

24. Douglas R. Edwards, "Heart," in *Harper's Bible Dictionary,* ed. Paul J. Achtemeier (San Francisco: Harper & Row, 1985), 377.

25. Henri J. M. Nouwen, *The Road to Daybreak: A Spiritual Journey* (New York: Doubleday Image Books, 1990), 47–48.

26. Annice Callahan, "Heart," in *The New Dictionary of Catholic Spirituality,* ed. Michael Downey (Collegeville, Minn.: Liturgical Press, 1993), 468–69.

27. Fran Ferder, *Words Made Flesh: Scripture, Psychology and Human Communication* (Notre Dame, Ind.: Ave Maria Press, 1995), 39.

28. Josephine A. Dolan, *Nursing in Society: A Historical Perspective* (Philadelphia: W. B. Saunders, 1973), 47.

29. Henri J. M. Nouwen, *Adam, God's Beloved* (Maryknoll, N.Y.: Orbis Books, 1997), 127.

30. Mary Elizabeth O'Brien, *Anatomy of a Nursing Home: A New View of Resident Life* (Owings Mills, Md.: National Health Publishing, 1989).

31. Henri J. M. Nouwen, *Reaching Out: The Three Movements of the Spiritual Life* (New York: Doubleday Image Books, 1986), 92.

32. Ibid., 93.

33. James D. Watkins, *Manual of Prayers* (Chicago, Ill.: Midwest Theological Forum, 1998), 251–52.

34. Douglas R. Edwards, "Hand," in *Harper's Bible Dictionary,* ed. Paul J. Achtemeier (San Francisco: Harper & Row, 1985), 371.

35. Ibid., 372.

36. Virginia Henderson, "The Nature of Nursing," *American Journal of Nursing* 64:1 (1964): 62–68, p. 63.

37. M. Basil Pennington, *Lectio Divina: Renewing the Ancient Practice of Praying the Scriptures* (New York: Crossroad, 1998).

38. Ibid., 51.

CHAPTER 4: THROUGH RAGING WATERS

1. Richard Sparks, "Suffering," in *The New Dictionary of Catholic Spirituality,* ed. Michael Downey (Collegeville, Minn.: Liturgical Press, 1993), 950–53, p. 950.

2. Ibid., 950.

3. Mary Ann Fatula, "Suffering," in *The New Dictionary of Theology*, eds. Joseph Komonchak, Mary Collins and Dermot Lane (Collegeville, Minn.: Liturgical Press, 1990), 990–92, p. 990.

4. Ibid., 991.

5. William Marravee, "A Christian Response to Suffering," *Review for Religious* 46:2 (1987): 256–60, p. 257.

6. Ibid., 259.

7. Dom Hubert van Zeller, *Suffering in Other Words* (Springfield, Ill.: Templegate, 1964), 20.

8. Ibid., 20.

9. P. A. Feider, *Arise and Walk: The Christian Search for Meaning in Suffering* (Notre Dame, Ind.: Fides/Claretian, 1980), 75–76.

10. Patrick Reilly, "The Scandal of Suffering," *New Blackfriars* 72:854 (1991): 461–68, pp. 464–65.

11. Rosemarie Carfagna, "A Spirituality of Suffering," *Review for Religious* 47:2 (1988), 255–63, p. 255.

12. Carla Johnson, "Coping with Compassion Fatigue," *Nursing '92* 4 (1992): 116–21, p. 121.

13. Hannah Hurnard, *Hinds' Feet on High Places* (Wheaton, Ill.: Tyndale House, 1975), 189.

14. Henri J. M. Nouwen, *Lifesigns: Intimacy, Fecundity and Ecstasy in Christian Perspective* (New York: Doubleday Image Books, 1989), 15.

15. Brother Roger of Taize, *No Greater Love: Sources of Taize*, (Collegeville, Minn.: Liturgical Press, 1991), 7.

16. Macrina Wiederkehr, *A Tree Full of Angels: Seeing the Holy in the Ordinary* (HarperSanFrancisco, 1995), 26.

17. Richard D. Parry, "Death, Dignity and Morality," *America* 179:15 (1998): 20–21, p. 21.

18. James Cardinal Hickey, "Alzheimer's Takes a Friend Away," *Catholic Standard* (Washington, D.C.: Archdiocese of Washington, September 24, 1998), 5.

19. Ibid.

20. Ibid.

21. Sandy Focht, "Dignity Entrusted" (letter to the editor), *America* 179:20 (1998): 26.

22. Brother Roger of Taize, *No Greater Love,* 7.

23. Henri J. M. Nouwen, *The Wounded Healer* (Garden City, N.Y.: Doubleday Image Books, 1979), 82.

24. Bernice Golberg, "Connection: An Exploration of Spirituality in Nursing Care, *Journal of Advanced Nursing* 27 (1998): 836–42, p. 838.

25. Judith Allen Shelly and Sharon Fish, *Spiritual Care: The Nurse's Role,* 3rd ed. (Downer's Grove, Ill.: InterVarsity Press, 1988), 101.

26. Ibid.

27. Kathy Kalina, *Midwife for Souls: Spiritual Care of the Dying* (Boston, Mass.: St. Paul Books and Media, 1993), 84.

28. Ralph DiOrio, *Called to Heal: Releasing the Transforming Power of God* (Garden City, N.Y.: Doubleday, 1982), 125.

CHAPTER 5: WITH EAGLES' WINGS

1. Monika Hellwig, "Hope," in *The New Dictionary of Catholic Spirituality,* ed. Michael Downey (Collegeville, Minn.: Liturgical Press, 1993), 506–15, p. 506.

2. Judith Allen Shelly and Arlene B. Miller, *Called to Care: A Christian Theology of Nursing* (Downers Grove, Ill.: InterVarsity Press, 1999), 149.

3. *The Liturgy of the Hours* (New York: Catholic Book Publishing Company, 1976), 432.

4. Ibid., 433.

5. Carroll Stuhlmueller, *The Gospel of Saint Luke* (Collegeville, Minn.: Liturgical Press, 1964), 151.

6. Jerome Kodell, *The Gospel According to Luke* (Collegeville, Minn.: Liturgical Press, 1989), 118.

7. Ibid.

8. Ibid., 119.

9. Donald Senior, Mary Ann Getty, Carroll Stuhlmueller and John J. Collins, The Catholic Study Bible (New American Bible) (New York: Oxford University Press, 1990), New Testament p. 63, note 46.

10. Ibid., Old Testament p. 658, note 1.

11. Ibid., Old Testament p. 658.

12. Diane Bergant, "The Wisdom Books," in The Catholic Study Bible (New American Bible), eds. Donald Senior, Mary Ann Getty, Carroll Stuhlmueller and John J. Collins (New York: Oxford University Press, 1990), RG231–RG286, p. RG243.

13. Daniel J. Harrington, *The Gospel According to Matthew* (Collegeville, Minn.: Liturgical Press, 1991), 114.

14. Philip Van Linden, *The Gospel According to Mark* (Collegeville, Minn.: Liturgical Press, 1991), 87.

15. Ibid.

16. Senior et al., New Testament p. 180, notes 26–27.

17. Neal Flanagan, *The Gospel According to John and the Johannine Epistles* (Collegeville, Minn.: Liturgical Press, 1989), 83.

18. J. H. Wright, "Prayer," in *The New Dictionary of Catholic Spirituality,* ed. Michael Downey (Collegeville, Minn.: Liturgical Press, 1993), 764–75, p. 764.

19. Miriam Pollard, *The Laughter of God: At Ease with Prayer* (Wilmington, Del.: Michael Glazier, 1986, 54–55.

20. Gerald May, *The Awakened Heart: Opening Yourself to the Love You Need* (San Francisco: HarperSanFrancisco, 1991), 171.

21. Elizabeth A. Livingstone, ed., *The Concise Oxford Dictionary of the Christian Church* (New York: Oxford University Press, 1990), 115.

22. David B. Guralnik, ed., *Webster's New World Dictionary,* 2nd college ed. (Cleveland: William Collins, 1980), 268.

23. Joann G. Widerquist, "Florence Nightingale's Calling," *Second Opinion* 17:3 (1992): 119, cited in Judith A. Shelly, "Is Prayer Unprofessional (editorial), *Journal of Christian Nursing* 12:1 (1995): 3.

24. Daughters of Charity, *Daughters of Charity Vocation Program* (video), (Emmitsburg, Md.: Daughters of Charity, 1993).

25. Marie Anne Mayeski, ed., *A Rocking-Horse Catholic: A Caryll Houselander Reader* (Kansas City, Mo.: Sheed & Ward, 1991), 93.

CHAPTER 6: WHERE YOUR TREASURE IS

1. Henri J. M. Nouwen, *Reaching Out: The Three Movements of the Spiritual Life* (New York: Doubleday Image Books, 1986), 73.

2. *Webster's Third New International Dictionary of the English Language,* unabridged, ed., Philip B. Gove (Springfield, Mass.: G. and C. Merriam Company, 1967), 1996.

3. Elizabeth A. Livingstone, *The Concise Oxford Dictionary of the Christian Church* (New York: Oxford University Press, 1990), 452.

4. Kevin W. Irwin, "Sacrament," in *The New Dictionary of Theology,* eds. Joseph A. Komonchak, Mary Collins and Dermot Lane (Collegeville, Minn.: Liturgical Press, 1990), 910–22, p. 910.

5. Gerald G. May, *The Awakened Heart: Opening Yourself to the Love You Need* (San Francisco: Harper, 1991), 73.

6. William L. Droel, *The Spirituality of Work: Nurses* (Chicago, Ill.: ACTA Publications, 1995), 11.

7. Ibid.

8. Mary Elizabeth O'Brien, *Living with HIV: Experiment in Courage* (Westport, Conn.: Auburn House, 1992), 99.

9. *Webster's Seventh New Collegiate Dictionary* (Springfield, Mass.: Merriam-Webster, 1976), 757.

10. Michael Downey, ed., *The New Dictionary of Catholic Spirituality* (Collegeville, Minn.: Liturgical Press, 1993), 845.

11. Donald Senior and Pheme Perkins, "The Gospels and Acts," in The Catholic Study Bible, New American Bible, eds. Donald Senior, Mary Ann Getty, Carroll Stuhlmueller and John J. Collins (New York: Oxford University Press, 1990), RG386–RG469, p. RG430.

12. Jerome Kodell, *The Gospel According to Luke* (Collegeville, Minn.: Liturgical Press, 1989), 62.

13. Kathy Schoonover-Shoffner, "A Call to Servanthood," *Journal of Christian Nursing* 14:4 (1997): 13–17, 37; p. 37.

14. M. Basil Pennington, *Lectio Divina, Renewing the Ancient Practice of Praying the Scriptures* (New York: Crossroad, 1998), 86.

15. Ibid.

16. Lawrence Boadt, "The Pentateuch," in The Catholic Study Bible, New American Bible, eds. Donald Senior, Mary Ann Getty,

Carroll Stuhlmueller and John J. Collins (New York: Oxford University Press, 1990), RG36–RG115, p. RG69.

17. David Alexander and Pat Alexander, eds., *Eerdmans' Handbook to the Bible* (Grand Rapids, Mich.: Eerdmans, 1983), 141.

18. James Carroll, "The Story of Abraham," in *Genesis: As It Is Written,* ed. David Rosenberg (New York: Harper, 1996), 73.

19. Henry Wansbrough, *Genesis: Doubleday Bible Commentary* (New York: Doubleday, 1998), 22.

20. Lawrence Boadt, *Reading the Old Testament: An Introduction* (Mahwah, N.J.: Paulist Press, 1984), 669.

CHAPTER 7: THAT THEY MAY HAVE LIFE

1. *Webster's Third New International Dictionary, Unabridged* (Springfield Mass.: G. & C. Merriam Company, 1967), 1942.

2. Ibid.

3. Thomas C. O'Brien, "Reverence," in *Encyclopedic Dictionary of Religion,* vol. *O–Z,* eds. Paul K. Meagher, Thomas C. O'Brien and Sister Consuelo M. Aherne (Washington, D.C.: Corpus Publications, 1979), 3040.

4. W. Herbst, "Reverence," in *New Catholic Encyclopedia,* vol. 12 (New York: McGraw-Hill, 1967), 448–49, p. 448.

5. Robert W. Hovda, "Reverence," in *The New Dictionary of Sacramental Worship,* ed. Peter E. Fink (Collegeville, Minn.: Liturgical Press, 1990), 1098–1100, p. 1098.

6. John Paul II, *Encyclical Letter, Evangelium Vitae, The Gospel of Life* (Boston, Mass.: Pauline Books and Media, March 25, 1995), 140.

7. Ibid., 73.

8. Ibid., 140.

9. Ibid., 153.

10. U.S. Catholic Bishops, "Living The Gospel of Life: A Challenge to American Catholics," *Origins, CNS Documentary Service* 28:25 (1998): 430–37, p. 435.

11. Mother Mary Aidan, *Reverence as an Effect of the True Concept of the Dignity of Man* (unpublished dissertation, Washington, D.C.: The Catholic University of America, 1952), 23.

12. Ibid., 33.

13. Ibid., 27.

14. *Catechism of the Catholic Church* (Liguori, Mo.: Liguori Publications, 1994), no. 1931.

15. Albert Schweitzer, *Reverence for Life,* trans. Reginald H. Fuller (New York: Harper & Row, 1969), 117.

16. John R. Stacer, "Divine Reverence for Us: God's Being Present, Cherishing and Persuading," *Theological Studies* 44:3 (1983): 438–55.

17. Josephine A. Dolan, *Nursing in Society: A Historical Perspective* (Philadelphia: W. B. Saunders, 1973), 56.

18. M. Adelaide Nutting and Lavinia L. Dock, *A History of Nursing,* vol. 1 (New York: G. P. Putnam's Sons, 1935), 230.

19. Mary Elizabeth O'Brien, *Spirituality in Nursing: Standing on Holy Ground* (Sudbury, Mass.: Jones and Bartlett, 1999), 37–52.

20. (1953). "The Nurse's Mass," *The Catholic Nurse* 2:2 (1953): 54–55, p. 54.

21. Ibid.

22. Ibid., 55.

23. Mother M. Virginia, "The Christlike Nurse," *The Catholic Nurse* 15:2 (1966): 46–51, 71; p. 48.

24. Pius XII, "The Holy Father Speaks to Nurses," *The Catholic Nurse* 1:1 (1952): 11–13, p. 12.

25. Ibid.

26. William W. Rankin, "Reverence For Life," *Journal of Pediatric Nursing* 4:3 (1989): 214–15, p. 214.

27. Anne Perry, "Reverence," *R.N.* 60:5 (1997): 39–40.

28. Kathy Kalina, *Midwife for Souls: Spiritual Care for the Dying* (Boston: St. Paul Books and Media, 1993).

29. O'Brien, *Spirituality in Nursing.*

30. Perry, 40.

31. Jeanine Young-Mason, "Sophocles' *Antigone* as a Source of Understanding Reverence for the Dead," *Nursing Forum* 22:4 (1985): 146–48, pp. 147–48.

32. Ibid., 148.

33. M. Baly, ed., *As Miss Nightingale Said...Florence .Nightingale Through Her Sayings—A Victorian Perspective* (London: Scutari Press, 1991), 68.

34. Minnie Goodnow, *Outlines of Nursing History* (Philadelphia: W. B. Saunders, 1916), 17.

35. Alice L. Price, *The Art, Science and Spirit of Nursing* (Philadelphia: W. B. Saunders, 1954), 3.

36. Richard Cardinal Cushing, "Comforters of the Afflicted," *The Catholic Nurse* 9:3 (1961): 22–24, p. 22.

37. Faye G. Abdellah and Eugene Levine, *Better Patient Care Through Nursing Research* (New York: Macmillan, 1979), 370.

38. Verna Benner Carson, "Nursing, Science and Service: A Historical Perspective," in *Spiritual Dimensions of Nursing Practice,* ed. Verna B. Carson (Philadelphia: W. B. Saunders, 1989), 52–73, p. 53.

39. Kathryn S. Bizek, "The Patient's Experience with Critical Illness," in *Critical Care Nursing: A Holistic Approach, 7th ed.,* eds. Carolyn M. Hudak, Barbara M. Gallo and Patricia G. Morton (Philadelphia: Lippincott, 1998), 9–20, p. 18.

40. Marlene A. Reimer, Barbara Tomlinson and Cathryn Bradshaw, *The Clinical Rotation Handbook: A Practicum Guide for Nurses* (Albany, N.Y.: Delmar, 1999), 11.

41. Ibid.

42. Judith Allen Shelly and Arlene B. Miller, *Called to Care: A Christian Theology of Caring* (Downer's Grove, Ill.: InterVarsity Press, 1999), 16.

43. David Alexander and Pat Alexander, *Eerdmans' Handbook to the Bible* (Grand Rapids, Mich.: William B. Eerdmans, 1992), 169.

44. Michael S. Driscoll, "Friendship," in *The New Dictionary of Catholic Spirituality,* ed. Michael Downey (Collegeville, Minn.: Liturgical Press, 1993), 423.

45. Ibid., 424.

46. Jerome Kodell, *The Gospel According to Luke* (Collegeville: Minn.: Liturgical Press, 1989), 9.

47. O'Brien, *Spirituality in Nursing,* 12.

48. Daniel J. Harrington, *The Gospel According to Matthew* (Collegeville, Minn.: Liturgical Press, 1991), 102.

49. Frank J. Matera, "Servant," in *Harper's Bible Dictionary*, ed. Paul J. Achtemeier (New York: Harper & Row, 1985), 929–30, p. 930.

50. Helen Doohan, "Service," in *The New Dictionary of Catholic Spirituality*, ed. Michael Downey (Collegeville, Minn.: Liturgical Press, 1993), 875.

51. Bruce J. Malina, "Service," in *Harper's Bible Dictionary*, ed. Paul J. Achtemeier (New York: Harper & Row, 1985), 930.

52. Philip Van Linden, *The Gospel According to Mark* (Collegeville, Minn.: Liturgical Press, 1983), 60.

CHAPTER 8: IN THE POTTER'S HANDS

1. Florence Nightingale, *Notes on Nursing: What It Is and What It Is Not* (London: Hamson, Bookseller to the Queen, 1859), 71.

2. Lawrence Boadt, *Jeremiah 1 to 25* (Collegeville, Minn.: Liturgical Press, 1991), xii.

3. Ibid.

4. Guy P. Couturier, "Jeremiah," in *The Jerome Biblical Commentary*, eds. Raymond E. Brown, Joseph A. Fitzmyer and Roland Murphy (Englewood Cliffs, N.J.: Prentice-Hall, 1968), 300–336, p. 317.

5. Peter F. Ellis, *Jeremiah, Baruch* (Collegeville, Minn.: Liturgical Press, 1986), 45.

6. Xavier Leon-Dufour, *Dictionary of the New Testament,* 2nd ed., trans. Terrance Prendergast (San Francisco: Harper & Row, 1980), 329.

7. C. Lattey, "Jeremias," in *A Catholic Commentary of Holy Scripture,* eds. Bernard Orchard, Edmund F. Sutcliffe, Reginald C. Fuller and Ralph Russell (New York: Thomas Nelson & Sons, 1953), 579.

8. (The fathers of the church), *Origen: Homilies on Jeremiah; Homilies on 1 Kings 28,* trans. John Clark Smith (Washington, D.C.: The Catholic University of America Press, 1998), 193.

9. Elizabeth Canham, *Journaling with Jeremiah* (Mahwah, N.J.: Paulist Press, 1992), 34.

10. Carlo Carretto, *Summoned by Love* (Maryknoll, N.Y.: Orbis Books, 1978), 127.

11. Roger S. Boraas, "Wheel," in *Harper's Bible Dictionary,* ed. Paul J. Achtemeier (New York: Harper & Row, 1985), 1132.

12. Jean-Pierre de Caussade, *Abandonment to Divine Providence,* trans. John Beevers (New York: Doubleday Image Books, 1975), 82.

13. Kay Wagoner, "A Nurse's Spin on the Potter's Wheel," *Journal of Christian Nursing* 13:4 (1996): 16–17, p. 16.

14. Ibid., 17.

15. Marilyn M. Straub, "Pottery," in *Harper's Bible Dictionary,* ed. Paul J. Achtemeier (New York: Harper & Row, 1985), 810–15, p. 810.

16. Ibid.

17. Paul J. Achtemeier, "Clay," in *Harper's Bible Dictionary,* ed. Paul J. Achtemeier (New York: Harper & Row, 1985), 173–74, p. 173.

18. Charlotte F. Speight and John Toki, *Hands in Clay: An Introduction to Ceramics,* 4th ed. (Mountain View, Calif.: Mayfield, 1999), 21.

19. Mary Elizabeth O'Brien, *Spirituality in Nursing: Standing on Holy Ground* (Sudbury, Mass.: Jones and Bartlett, 1999), 7–8.

20. M. Patricia Donahue, *Nursing: The Finest Art: An Illustrated History* (St. Louis, Mo.: C. V. Mosby, 1996).

21. Duane L. Christensen, "Fire," in *Harper's Bible Dictionary,* ed. Paul J. Achtemeier (New York: Harper & Row, 1985), 309.

22. Robert A. Coughenour, "Furnace," in *Harper's Bible Dictionary* ed. Paul J. Achtemeier (New York: Harper & Row, 1985), 323–24, p. 324.

23. Hannah Hurnard, *Hinds' Feet on High Places* (Wheaton, Ill.: Tyndale House), 85 (emphasis added).

24. Ibid., 90 (emphasis added).

25. Henri J. M. Nouwen, *The Wounded Healer* (Garden City, N.Y.: Doubleday Image Books, 1979), 81–96.

26. Jerome I. Rodale, *The Synonym Finder* (Emmaus, Pa.: Rodale Press, 1978), 1316.

27. Phyllis A. Bird, "Vessel," in *Harper's Bible Dictionary,* ed. Paul J. Achtemeier (New York: Harper & Row, 1985), 1111.

28. Straub, 813.

29. Henri J. M. Nouwen, *Bread for the Journey* (HarperSanFrancisco, 1997), 13–16.